# a greener Christmas

EDITOR-IN-CHIEF

## SHEHERAZADE GOLDSMITH

**LONDON • NEW YORK**
**MELBOURNE • MUNICH • DELHI**

**Photography** Peter Anderson
**Crafters** Barbara Coupe,
Francine Raymond, Lucy Harrington,
Ted & Harry, Made in Hastings, Sparrowkids

**Project Editor** Susannah Steel
**Project Designer** John Round

**FOR DORLING KINDERSLEY**
**Project Art Editor and Designer** Caroline de Souza
**Project Editor** Laura Nickoll
**Photographic Art Direction** Caroline de Souza
**Editorial Assistant** Andrew Roff
**Senior Jacket Creative** Nicola Powling
**Managing Editor** Dawn Henderson
**Managing Art Editor** Christine Keilty
**Production Editor** Ben Marcus
**Production Controller** Wendy Penn

First American Edition, 2008

Published in the United States by DK Publishing
375 Hudson Street, New York, New York 10014
08 09 10 11   10 9 8 7 6 5 4 3 2 1

AD402—08/2008

A catalog record for this book is available from the Library of Congress

ISBN 978-0-7566-3693-7

DK books are available at special discounts when purchased in bulk for
sales promotions, premiums, fund-raising, or educational use.
For details, contact: DK Publishing Special Markets, 375 Hudson Street, New
York, New York 10014 or SpecialSales@dk.com.

Color reproduction by MDP, UK

Printed and bound in China by Sheck Wah Tong

Discover more at **www.dk.com**

# CONTENTS

# TABLE

# FOOD

# Introduction

I love Christmas, or at least I love the ritual of it: buying a tree and enjoying the scent of pine in my house; carefully unwrapping last year's decorations, and hanging stockings; the soft twinkle of Christmas lights in the windows; and mince pies and hampers from friends that are filled with delicious goodies. But above all, I love Christmas because my kids love it.

The reasons why my kids love Christmas differ, of course, from mine. Their love of Christmas is not a nostalgic one, as mine is, but comes from the excitement of building up to a day that is full of anticipation and hope— a time that is about preparation, creating and baking, of vast family gatherings, fleeting visits from godparents, of delicious sweet seasonal temptations and, most importantly of all for the kids, patiently coveted gifts. All of these things have one thing in common, and that is they all require a little time and effort. In my mind, it is this pure, and as yet untainted, view that young children have that is the very essence of Christmas.

**"This book is the antithesis of that instant last-minute Christmas Eve dash through the crowds to the stores"**

## The commercial reality

Somehow this day that should be full of creativity, good will, and thoughtfulness has lost its way and has ended up as a symbol of our throw-away society, in which we buy products that have no real use, are not designed to last and, despite their huge, long-lasting polluting production costs, provide only a brief thrill. Christmas Eve and Christmas Day are now widely recognized as the two most polluting days of the year: the equivalent of three weeks of carbon dioxide emissions and three billion tons of extra garbage are

generated worldwide over this short period. Much of the extra trash collected contains discarded gifts, most of which will end up in landfill sites.

**"Make your impact on the world as a consumer at Christmas time a positive one"**

Container ships are also now carrying record volumes of cheap, Christmas consumer goods from China—all of which are expected to have a life span of less than four months. Relying on chain stores for all your Christmas needs and throwing all your garbage out in one bag will save time over the festive season, but choosing token presents without much thought seems, to me, to contradict its meaning.

## Positive solutions

This book is about having a simpler, more home-spun Christmas. It's about giving home-crafted presents, making your own decorations, and festive baking. It's about rethinking and changing the way you consume

and recycle. Every purchase you make, whether it be an Advent calendar or the ingredients for your Christmas dinner, has either a direct or an indirect effect on your own health, on human and animal welfare, and on the environment. By choosing to buy—wherever possible—organic, fairly traded, locally produced, sustainably sourced, biodegradable, or recyclable goods, you are effectively making your impact on the world a positive one. We are getting very good at recycling, but it is easy to be overwhelmed by the sheer mass of waste generated at Christmas. The good news is that most things, including your Christmas tree, Christmas cards, and wrapping paper, are

**"I hope this book will inspire you to take on a different approach to Christmas, and spare you the stress"**

recyclable. In fact, according to one statistic, "If everything in the trash can was recycled, it would save enough energy to fly Santa Claus in a plane around the world 64,500 times."

## Reclaiming the spirit of Christmas

I hope this book will inspire you to take a different approach to Christmas, and spare you the stress of excess consumerism. Whether it's creating your own unique Christmas tree decorations from garden finds or kitchen ingredients, putting together a hamper full of delicious homemade treats, or making a special gift, there is no denying that Christmas is the perfect time to change old habits and make a positive contribution to the environment. There is something very personal and satisfying about making your own presents, and the most heartfelt compliments and thank yous I have ever received from people have been for gift hampers like the ones in this book, which I fill with homemade jams, chutneys, and cakes. This book includes a wide range of other fantastic gift ideas too, such as natural remedies and vintage-inspired "must haves." Most of the projects in this book are simple enough for anyone to do, and many are extremely child-friendly and may involve lots of kitchen and gluing chaos!

**So good luck, and Merry Christmas.**

*S. Goldsmith*

# Make a dried leaf wreath

★ ★ ☆  LEVEL OF DIFFICULTY

Dressing your front door with a wreath at Christmas time helps to create a wonderfully warm, festive welcome to your home. The only downside is that you can't enjoy the wreath indoors. The solution is to hang another, more delicate, decorative wreath in your living room or hallway: collect fallen leaves and seed heads in the fall and turn them into this stunning arrangement.

## materials

- Richly colored leaves
- Sheets of newspaper
- 1 large circular wire wreath frame, available from florists or mail-order companies
- Thin wire
- Mesh ribbon
- Eco-friendly adhesive glue

### 🍃 Craft tip

**Collecting leaves**
Look for fallen leaves in early and mid-fall before the weather takes its toll. Red oak (*Quercus rubra*) and maple (*Acer*) are good choices. Depending on the room temperature and type of leaf, they can take up to a week to dry out and flatten.

**1** Arrange leaves in a single layer between sheets of newspaper under a mat or piece of carpet, or place a couple of heavy books on top.

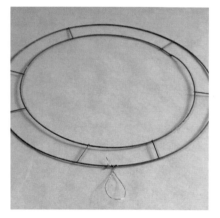

**2** Once the flattened leaves are completely dry, make up the wreath. Secure the wire in a loop and attach it to the top of the frame.

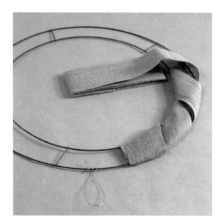

**3** Wrap the mesh ribbon around the frame in a zig-zag fashion. Staple it onto the frame at intervals to cover the frame completely.

**4** Glue large leaves onto the mesh, stems pointing inward, so that they overlap slightly. Glue small leaves on top in an even pattern. Allow to dry.

# Plant a winter garden

Scented plants and shrubs with richly colored berries and leaves keep a garden looking alive and interesting during the long winter months. The beauty of growing well-chosen, fully-hardy plants at this time of year is that you can cut fresh stems and sprigs from the plants to decorate and scent your home. The berries, fruits, and ground cover will also attract and support wildlife.

## Scented plants

• *Mahonia japonica* is an upright, evergreen shrub with dark-green, sharply toothed leaves that turn scarlet in fall. From late fall to early spring it has spikes of fragrant yellow flowers with a scent similar to Lily-of-the-valley.

• Chinese witch hazel (*Hamamelis mollis*) is a deciduous shrub with extremely fragrant clusters of large, golden-yellow flowers on its bare branches in mid- and late winter.

• *Viburnum* x *bodnantense* 'Dawn' is another deciduous, upright shrub with gray-blue leaves in summer that turn to red in fall. From October to March it has numerous, densely packed clusters of large, sweetly fragrant rose, pink or blush white flowers.

• The small, bushy, evergreen Christmas box (*Sarcococca confusa*) has long, slender, dark green leaves, tiny honey-scented, white winter flowers and black berries in spring.

## Plants with berries

• The deciduous Beauty berry (*Callicarpa bodinieri* var. *giraldii* 'Profusion') has small but striking clusters of violet berries with bronze-purple foliage in fall.

• The single-flowering hybrid *Rosa rugosa* var *alba* bears large, plump, orange hips in winter.

• *Gaultheria mucronata* 'Wintertime', an evergreen, female shrub, must be grown in groups with *Gaultheria mucronata* 'Thymifolia' to grow its round white winter berries.

• The evergreen holly (*Ilex aquifolium* 'J.C. van Tol') has shiny dark-green leaves and bears lots of attractive red berries.

## Bulbs to plant

• *Allium cristophii* bulbs produce huge umbels of lilac-purple, star-shaped flowers about 12 in (30 cm) high in the summer that retain their color until fall. Once the color has disappeared, they keep their structure through winter, turning almost silvery. Plant in fall, about 3 in (8 cm) deep. They will grow anywhere, in any soil, but prefer full sun.

• *Cyclamen coum* has fuschia-pink flowers and variably patterned silver and green leaves. It flowers in late winter. Plant bulbs about 2 in (5 cm) deep in partial shade.

• Stinking iris (*Iris foetidissima*) produces attractive pods of scarlet seeds which open in fall and remain all winter. It grows 30 in (75 cm) high and likes sun or shade and damp or dry conditions. Plant bulbs about 2 in (5 cm) deep.

• Snowdrop (*Galanthus* 'S. Arnott') is a vigorous, honey-scented variety with pendant white flowers that bloom in late winter. Plant the bulbs 2 in (5 cm) deep in sun or partial shade in moist soil that doesn't dry out in summer.

# Winter plant varieties

*Gaultheria mucronata* 'Wintertime' Needs acidic, preferably peaty soil and likes partial shade, although will fruit best in sun.

*Rosa rugosa* **var. *alba*** Prefers an open, sunny site and needs fertile, moist, but well-drained soil.

**Holly (*Ilex aquifolium* J.C. van Tol')** Grows in moist, well-drained, moderately fertile, humus-rich soil in full sun or partial shade.

**Beauty Berry (*Callicarpa bodinieri* var. *giraldii* 'Profusion')** Grows best in full sun and fertile, well-drained soil.

*Mahonia japonica* Grows in moderately fertile, humus-rich, moist, but well-drained soil in partial shade, or sun if the soil is moist.

*Viburnum x bodnantense* 'Dawn' Grows in moderately fertile, moist but well-drained soil in full sun or partial shade.

Chinese witch hazel *(Hamamelis mollis)* Flourishes in sun or semi-shade and moderately fertile, moist but well-drained soil.

Christmas box *(Sarcococca confusa)* Grows in moderately fertile, humus-rich, moist but well-drained soil in deep or partial shade.

# Fabric garland

★★★  LEVEL OF DIFFICULTY

This charming garland is versatile enough to decorate mantlepieces, kitchen dressers, Christmas trees, and bedrooms. Store it carefully and it can be reused every year. You can make your own felt by washing an old, unwanted, cream-colored 100 percent wool blanket or garment in a hot machine wash. You'll need brown felt for the gingerbread man.

## materials

- Garland templates (pp.314–17)
- Large piece of cream-colored felt
- Brown felt for the gingerbread man
- Scissors
- Pins
- Eco-friendly marker pen
- Colored embroidery thread (for blanket stitching and features) and needle
- Ricrac trimming
- 5 lengths of wire, each about 3 in (8 cm) long
- 3 ft (1 m) twine or string
- Pieces of recycled ribbon
- Old, unwanted woollen garment or scarf
- Recycled buttons

**1** Cut and pin together two of each shape from cream felt, and two gingerbread men from brown felt. Decorate one stocking with the pen.

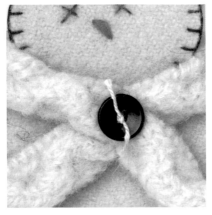

**2** Sew the shapes together. Leave the mitten and stocking tops unsewn. Sew on the features and ricrac trimming (see pp.30–31).

**3** Thread a piece of wire through the top of each shape and secure in a loop. Thread the twine through the loops and tie ribbons onto the twine.

**4** Cut strips from the garment for scarves and sew them, together with some decorative ribbons and buttons, onto the fabric shapes.

# Fabric garland variations

**Mitten** Sew a folded length of recycled ribbon and a vintage button on to the front of the mitten. Leave the top unstitched.

**Christmas tree** Cut two tree shapes *(p.316)* from green felt, sew them together, and decorate with ricrac trimming and buttons.

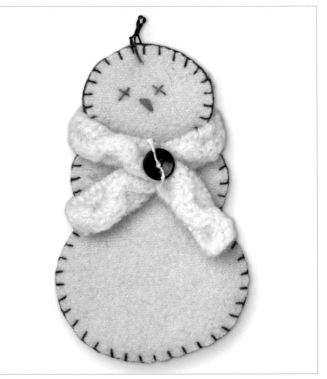

**Robin** Cut a circle of fabric *(p.317)*, fold in half, insert a fabric beak, and sew the curved edges together. Add wings and a red breast.

**Snowman** Sew two eyes and draw a carrot nose with a fabric pen, then attach a length of wool fabric as a scarf with a button.

**Stocking** Embroider simple details on to the toe and heel of the sock. Decorate with a folded length of ribbon and a button.

**Gingerbread man** Sew ricrac trimming on to the arms and feet, and cut out and sew on a scarf and button in jolly colors.

**Holly and berries** Cut two holly shapes *(p.325)* from plaid fabric, sew them together, insert a wire circle, and add red berry buttons.

**Candy cane** Wrap a small length of brightly colored ribbon around the stick and secure it in place with a sewn-on button.

# Make a wood fire

Burning wood has to be the most luxurious way to heat a room sustainably, and there's nothing more welcoming than the sight and smell of a real log fire. Wood is a carbon-neutral, renewable source of fuel, and it releases the same amount of carbon dioxide when burned as if it were to rot naturally. So it's a much better alternative to unenvironmentally friendly fossil fuels.

Recently cut wood tends to have a lot of water in it, so it can smoulder and burn inefficiently. Use firewood that has been cut, split, stored, and left to "season" for at least a year; the drier the wood, the more efficient the fire. Splitting logs and stacking them outside under a cover allows the air to circulate freely and dry the wood out sooner. Use hardwoods for firewood: they have a greater density of fibres and burn slower and longer. Good firewoods are beech, apple, pear, pine, and oak. Ash is considered the best for both firewood and kindling, but whichever wood you choose, buy it from sustainably managed sources. In the UK, look out for a FSC (Forest Stewardship Council) logo.

## Starting a wood fire

The more small, dry kindling you have, the more easily your fire will start; there's no need to use toxic chemical firelighters if your kindling and wood are dry. Scrunch up some sheets of newspaper fairly tightly and put them in the fire grate. Pile the kindling on top, criss-crossing it loosely so there is plenty of air between each piece; wood that is packed too tightly won't burn properly. Add two or three small pieces of firewood at the side and back of the kindling pile. Light the bottom of the newspaper at the front with a match, and the kindling should catch fire quite quickly. You need a good draft of air up the chimney to encourage the flames to pick up, so you may want to open a grate or window just to get the fire started. As the flames begin to subside, place a couple more pieces of wood on the kindling and allow the fire to become established.

## Home energy facts

- **Nearly £5 billion** of energy is wasted in the UK every year. More than 40 percent of all heat lost in an average home is lost through the loft space and walls. If everyone in the UK insulated their lofts with the recommended 11 in (27 cm) of insulation, it would save the UK the cost of building three large nuclear power stations.

- **By placing** a light-reflective material behind a radiator, you can reflect the heat back into the room and save up to $20 per radiator a year.

- **Turn your temperature** thermostat down by 2°F (1°C) to reduce your heating consumption by about ten percent a year.

- **Around 20 percent** of heat energy is lost through ventilation and drafts. Close your curtains at dusk to keep out cold drafts and stop heat escaping.

- **A crack as small** as $\frac{1}{6}$ in (2 mm) around a window can let in as much cold air as leaving the window open 3 in (8 cm), so check that your windows fit well.

# Scent a room

Delicately scented rooms are somehow more inviting, and the subtly uplifting aroma of a potpourri will make your home seem cosier. Collect a mixture of natural materials and aromatic spices, arrange them in your favorite bowl, and sprinkle over scented oils: the potpourri will look and smell lovely.

## Potpourri recipes

### • Spice potpourri
Collect a few cinnamon sticks, star anise, a nutmeg or two, some cloves, and a selection of dried natural materials or some walnuts and hazelnuts.

Sprinkle over 10 drops of cinnamon oil and 5 drops of clove oil.

### • Citrus potpourri
Dry some whole clementines, kumquats, orange and lemon slices, and orange and lemon peel.

Sprinkle over 10 drops of orange oil and 5 drops of lemon oil.

### • Pine potpourri
Collect the cones and a few small branches of any fragrant evergreens—pine, juniper, Cyprus, and so on.

Sprinkle over 10 drops of pine oil and 5 drops of cedar oil.

### • Garden potpourri
Gather a selection of natural materials such as thistles, berries, rosehips, and lavender and rosemary stems, and allow them to dry out throughly.

Sprinkle over 10 drops of lavender oil and 5 drops of rosemary oil.

Potpourri is made of three ingredients: dried natural materials, which comprise the filling, and spices and scented oils to create fragrance. The natural materials can include whatever you find visually pleasing and suit the type of potpourri you're making. Collect interesting seasonal flowers, seed heads, flower heads, fruits, sprigs of foliage, and berries. To dry these ingredients thoroughly, spread them in a single layer on newspaper and leave for a week or so in a warm, dry place out of the sun and away from draughts. Fruits like oranges, lemons, and kumquats need to be dried slightly differently: cover a wire rack with cheesecloth, place the whole fruits or fruit slices in a single layer on top and leave in the oven on a low temperature or in a cabinet for up to 48 hours (p.65).

## Making up a potpourri
Arrange the dried natural materials and spices in a large bowl and sprinkle a few drops of scented essential oil over them. Cover the potpourri in the bowl until needed and refresh with a few more drops of oil when necessary. Try mixing your own combination of scented oils to create a pleasing aroma, or follow a recipe (left).

## Scenting a room quickly
Other, quicker ways of creating scent include placing pine cones, orange peel, or seasoned apple wood on top of a wood fire as it burns, and placing a saucer of orange peel or lemon peel, or small bowls of water containing a few drops of scented oil, next to a warm radiator.

## Preparing for Christmas

If you have a well-ventilated outside shed or covered area, use it to store onions and other winter produce, and to hang any foliage for decorating the house, so that it all stays as fresh as possible.

# Grow a mistletoe shrub

The evergreen mistletoe plant has become an essential part of our Christmas tradition, and everyone loves its romantic connotations. The bushy shrub is actually a partial parasite that grows in the branches of old trees: it extracts essential nutrients and water by pushing its roots under the bark of the host tree. Although it is slow-growing and can be hard to establish, mistletoe is worth cultivating if you enjoy its clusters of smooth, bright green, oval leaves and waxy white berries in your home at Christmas time.

Mistletoe *(Viscum album)* reproduces naturally when birds —usually mistle thrushes—eat the berries and excrete the seeds onto the bark of a host tree, where they germinate. Popular host trees are those with soft bark, particularly apple trees, and also hawthorn, linden, and poplar trees. After attaching itself to the host, a young plant produces leaves after the first year; just two new branches with a pair of leaves at each tip grow every year.

## Propagating mistletoe

The best time to propagate mistletoe is between March and April, when the seeds are fully ripe. If you can't find fresh berries from a living plant, preserve some Christmas sprigs with berries in a jar of water in the window of a cold, frost-free room until the end of February. Use the sticky "glue" of the berry to attach it to the side or underside of an apple tree branch about 8 inches (20 cm) in diameter. The higher up a tree the branch is, and the more sunlight the plant gets, the better. Wind some wool or twine around the branch to mark the site and leave the plant to establish naturally. It's worth applying 15 or more berries to your host tree, as mistletoe requires male and female plants to produce berries. The germination rate is also quite low (only one in ten seeds becomes a plant), and some berries may fall off or be eaten by birds. It will take four to five years for the plant to produce berries.

To decorate your home with mistletoe, cut a few stems from the shrub with a pair of shears, bind the base of the stems with some twine, and hang the bundle from a ceiling light or above a doorway.

# Edible bird decorations

★ ★ ★  LEVEL OF DIFFICULTY

A garden full of wildlife is always an uplifting sight on a winter's day. To encourage birds into your garden, hang homemade birdseed balls from trees and shrubs. The birds rely on these additional sources of nutrients if natural foods are scarce, and in severe winter weather when snow is on the ground. Use a recycled glass tumbler as a mold if you don't have an old tennis ball.

## materials

- 18 oz (500 g) lard
- 3½ oz (100 g) coarse oats
- 3½ oz (100 g) nuts— peanuts are a good choice
- 3½ oz (100 g) dried fruits
- 3½ oz (100 g) seeds— sunflower seeds are the best choice
- Garden wire
- Old tennis ball or similar, sliced in half and with a small round hole cut out of the top, then resealed by wrapping a length of wire around the ball and twisting the wire ends together securely
- Garden string

**1** Put the lard into a saucepan and melt it gently over a low heat. While the lard is melting, mix the dry ingredients together.

**2** Add handfuls of the dry food to the melted lard and mix them together. The dry ingredients should all be well coated in the lard.

**3** Insert a piece of wire, which is a little longer than the mold, down through the center of the mold. Pack the seed mix in around the wire.

**4** Leave the seed mix in the molds to cool completely, then remove the molds, attach string to the wires, and hang the decorations up high.

# Welcome birds into a winter garden

Help birds to survive another season by giving them shelter, regular supplies of food (p.44), and drinking water through the cold winter months.

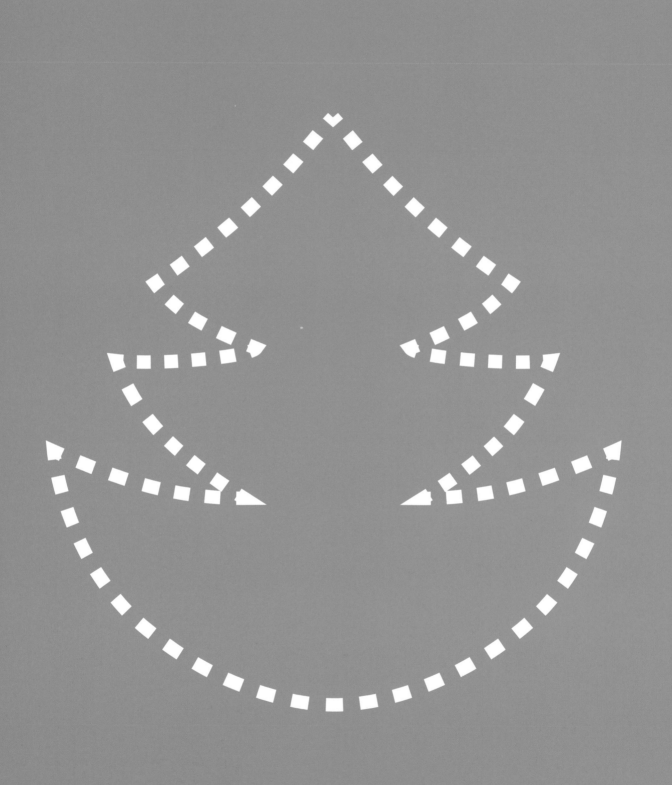

# CHRISTMAS
# TREE

# Buy and recycle a real tree

For many of us, a real tree trimmed with decorations is what Christmas is all about, and it takes pride of place in our homes. Looking after a cut Christmas tree properly will help to prolong its fresh scent and vibrant color, but just as important is knowing how to recycle the tree afterwards, because the benefits of recycling Christmas trees are enormous.

It takes tree farmers about ten years to produce a 10 ft (three-meter) Christmas tree, and some varieties can reach great heights if left to grow: the Nordman fir (Abies nordmanniana) can reach 13 ft (40 meters), for example. The best varieties to choose are Noble fir (Abies procera) and Nordman fir (Abies nordmanniana), as they have a good color and scent and hang on to their needles well, and Scots pine (Pinus sylvestris), which has the best scent.

## Choosing a tree

Buy a locally grown tree with a Christmas tree growers' association label (right) to ensure it has been sustainably grown: you'll be supporting your local grower and minimizing the impact of transport miles, and you can guarantee it has been freshly cut and its needles will stay on longer. Norway Spruce (Picea abies), the "original" Christmas tree, is mostly imported from Scandinavia and Holland and is cut down weeks before you buy it, which is why it sheds its needles quickly. Cut ¼–⅛ in (3–5 mm) off the base of your tree trunk, stand it in water, add a tablespoon of honey (which mimics the tree's sap), and keep the room as cool as possible to help the tree stay fresher for longer.

## Recycling your tree

We currently send almost all our cut trees to landfill sites, but recycled trees can be reduced to chippings and used to benefit the environment again as mulch, path surfacing, and soil improvers. Most councils now provide a collection point from which the trees will be properly pulped and recycled, or find out where your nearest recycling center is.

## Christmas tree facts

**According to the charity** Action for Sustainable Living, over six million cut trees were bought last year in the UK, but only 750,000—about 12.5 percent—were recycled. The rest created 9,000 tons of waste in landfill sites, and will take hundreds of years to biodegrade.

**In past years**, many trees were flown from elsewhere in Europe into the UK, but today a large number of trees are grown in British plantations. Approximately 30,000 acres of land yield eight million trees each year.

**When buying a tree in the UK**, check that it has the BCTGA (British Christmas Tree Growers Association) logo, which guarantees that it has been sustainably farmed.

**An artificial Christmas tree** may be reusable, but it will probably have been made from a petroleum-based product and may well have been flown in from China. The materials commonly used in the manufacture of artificial trees are PVC, polyurethane foam, and steel. Although you may reuse it for several years, if your tree is not recyclable it will eventually linger for centuries in a landfill site.

# Christmas tree in a pot

★ ★ ★    LEVEL OF DIFFICULTY

One of the great pleasures of Christmas is decorating a real tree, so why not buy a living tree with roots and plant it in a pot? A small tree makes a great table decoration. You can re-pot it, care for it through the seasons, and reuse it for several Christmases to come. If you live in the UK, buy a tree with a Forest Stewardship Council (FSC) accreditation from a small-scale sustainable grower.

## materials

- 1 dwarf conifer tree with the roots well soaked in a bucket of water; if you choose another variety, check on the eventual height of the tree before you buy it
- 1 container with draining holes
- Bark-based, coarse organic compost
- Watering can

### 🍃 Green tip

**Owning a living tree**
Don't keep the tree indoors for any longer than one month: the warmth and light may encourage it to break dormancy. Feed and water it regularly, re-pot into a larger container in early spring, and add some slow-release organic fertilizer, such as comfrey pellets.

**1** Tease the roots of the root ball to loosen them. Fill the base of the container with some compost and place the tree in the container.

**2** Pack the spaces around the root ball with more compost. Gently shake the container occasionally to distribute the compost evenly.

**3** Fill the container to just below the rim with some more compost, then firm the earth around the plant with your hands.

**4** Water the plant thoroughly to ensure that all the compost is wet, allow to drain, and then bring it indoors to decorate.

# Use energy-efficient lights

For many of us, Christmas lights on our trees, around our mantlepieces, and even in our gardens, are essential seasonal decorations. They create such a cozy, atmospheric glow that it's tempting to turn them on indoors during the day, as well as at nighttime. This helps to contribute to the fact that we curently consume much more energy at home over Christmas, which in turn has an impact on the environment and climate change. So it's worth switching to LED tree lights, and using energy-efficient light bulbs in your home.

If you leave a set of conventional Christmas tree lights on in your home for ten hours a day over the 12 days of Christmas, you'll produce enough carbon dioxide (one of the main greenhouse gases) to inflate 64 party balloons. Outdoor lights tend to use even more energy, since they are usually high-wattage and therefore less energy-efficient. However, it's easy to save energy and still enjoy a wonderful light display.

## LED lights

Light-emitting diode, or LED, Christmas tree lights emit a bright, vibrant light that uses 80 percent less energy than conventional tree lights. They are also longer-lasting and stay cooler than traditional bulbs because they don't have a filament. The brilliance of their color makes LED lights suitable for both indoor and outdoor use. Solar-powered lights are also a good choice, as even on a wintry day they can soak up enough sun to illuminate an indoor or outdoor Christmas tree without the need for an electricity supply

## Energy-saving light bulbs

Like LED lights, energy-saving bulbs use around a quarter of the electricity of standard bulbs, and last up to 12 times longer. Advances in technology mean that these bulbs are now sold in a range of fittings, shapes, and sizes. Look for government and industry-approved energy-saving logos to find the most energy-efficient products when you shop.

## Energy facts

**A household with** an extravagant Christmas light display will spend enough money to heat and power an average house for six weeks, and produce 882 lb (400 kg) of carbon dioxide—more than enough to fill two double-decker buses.

**Only ten percent** of the electricity used to light an ordinary light bulb is turned into light. The other 90 percent is wasted as heat.

**If every household** only used energy-efficient bulbs, enough energy could be saved to close several power plants.

**One energy-efficient** light bulb will save up to $14 and around 88 lb (40 kg) of carbon dioxide a year. And because it lasts up to 12 times longer, it could save around $120 before it needs replacing. These savings take into account the higher cost of energy-saving light bulbs.

**Recycle all energy-efficient** light bulbs safely, as they contain small amounts of mercury: wear gloves to pick up a bulb, put it in a plastic bag, and recycle it at a local recycling facility.

# Natural Christmas tree

Dried fruits (pp.64–65), spices (pp.60–61), and foraged materials (pp.58–59, 62–63) can be turned into stunning decorations that look rustic and smell wonderful.

# Christmas tree star

★ ☆ ☆   LEVEL OF DIFFICULTY

Select slender, flexible twigs for this tree-top decoration, and leave on any buds, catkins, or seed heads to add interest. To dry the leaves flat, arrange them in a single layer between sheets of newspaper and leave them for a week or so under a mat, or place a couple of heavy books on top. Arrange the flower heads on newspaper and leave them in a warm, dry place for a week as well.

## materials

- 5 twigs
- Star template *(p.323)*, roughly drawn on recycled cardboard
- Thin wire
- 3 richly colored, five-pointed dried leaves in different sizes
- Eco-friendly adhesive glue
- 5 dried flower heads

**1** Trim each of the twigs so that they are about 12 in (30 cm) in length. Remove the dried leaves and flower heads from the newspaper.

**2** Lay the card template on a flat surface. Arrange the twigs over the star drawn on the template so that they echo its shape.

### 🎄 Craft tip

**The best twigs to use**
Twigs from beech *(Fagus)*, hazel *(Corylus)*, willow *(Salix)*, dogwood *(Cornus)*, and birch *(Betula)* trees are best for this project. It's worth collecting the twigs just before you want to use them so that they are as supple as possible.

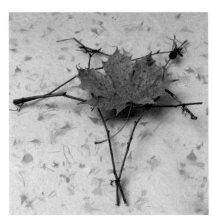

**3** Wind a piece of wire around the joint where two twigs meet in a point and secure the ends together. Repeat at the other four corners.

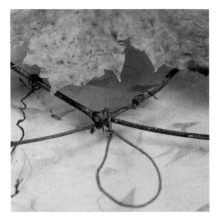

**4** Attach a wire loop to the top of the star frame. Glue the leaves onto the frame in order of size and glue the flower heads onto the back.

# Cinnamon spice bundles

★★★ LEVEL OF DIFFICULTY

With its distinctly warm, aromatic smell, cinnamon spice can instantly create a familiar festive scent in any room. Golden-red cinnamon sticks, which are actually pieces of bark from the evergreen cinnamon tree, are easy to purchase and make striking natural decorations. Try finding long cinnamon sticks to make these spice bundles for your Christmas tree.

**1** Secure the cinnamon sticks in a bundle with the elastic band. Thread the wire under the elastic band and secure it tightly in a loop.

**2** Thread a nutmeg onto the raffia, down to one end. Tie a knot in the end of the raffia to secure the nutmeg. Repeat at the other end.

**3** Wrap the raffia around the cinnamon bundle a couple of times so that the elastic band is completely hidden. Secure in a knot.

**4** Glue the star anise onto the front of the orange slice, then glue the orange slice onto the raffia so that it covers the knot.

## materials

**For each decoration**

- 6–8 cinnamon sticks
- 1 recycled elastic band
- Length of thin wire, approximately 6 in (15 cm) long
- 2 nutmegs with a hole drilled through the center of each (use a clamp and fine-bore drill bit)
- Length of recycled natural raffia, about 20 in (50 cm) long
- Eco-friendly adhesive glue
- 1 star anise
- 1 dried orange slice (p.65)

# Make Christmas lanterns

★ ★ ★  LEVEL OF DIFFICULTY

If you love foraging, you'll enjoy collecting the delicate natural materials required for these exquisite tree decorations. As well as gathering the papery red Chinese lanterns *(Physalis)* that appear in late summer and fall, look out for moss, rosehips *(Rosa)*, crab apples *(Malus)*, thistles *(Carlina)*, Old man's beard from clematis *(Ranunculaceae)*, and anything else that catches your eye.

## materials

### For each decoration

- 1 length of thin wire, approximately 12 in (30 cm) long
- 1 small piece of twig
- Knitting needle or skewer
- An assortment of found natural materials, including seed heads and small fruits with their stalks left on, and then dried *(p.16)*

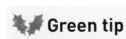 **Green tip**

### Eco-friendly products

If you want to mix your homemade tree decorations with some bought decorations, choose fairly traded and ethically sourced products that have been produced from sustainably grown, natural materials.

**1** Wrap one end of the length of wire around around the small piece of twig a few times and secure the end neatly.

**2** Use a knitting needle or a skewer to pierce a hole through a crab apple fruit or a berry, as close to the centre as possible.

**3** Thread the wire through the fruit, then push it carefully through the Chinese lantern. Make a knot in the wire below the lantern.

**4** Wrap the remaining wire around the stems of a thistle and a seed head, leaving enough wire at the end to secure in a loop.

# Spiced orange decorations

★ ★ ★   LEVEL OF DIFFICULTY

Even after they have been dried thoroughly, oranges retain enough of an aroma to fill a room for many days with their citrus scent. Their mellow orange hues and cylindrical shape also means that they make naturally attractive decorations, especially when hung from the vibrant green branches of a real conifer tree.

## materials

**For each decoration**

- Eco-friendly adhesive glue
- 1 star anise
- 1 dried orange slice
- 1 flat, dried bay leaf
- Several lengths of thin wire
- A handful of cloves
- 1 dried, whole clementine
- Skewer or knitting needle
- 1 cinnamon stick

**1** Glue the star anise onto the front of the orange slice, and the bay leaf onto the back. Secure a length of wire in a loop at the top of the orange.

**2** Stick cloves into the clementine in a pattern. Push a skewer through the fruit, thread wire through the hole and secure one end in a loop.

**3** Thread wire lengthways through the cinnamon stick. Bend one end over, thread the other end through the clementine loop, and secure.

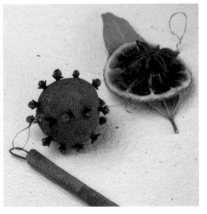

**4** Attach the loose wire at the top of the clementine to the orange slice. The three parts should now all be joined together by wire.

### 🍃 Craft tip

**Dehydrating fruits**
Arrange the slices and whole fruits in a single layer on a piece of cheesecloth on a wire rack. Leave to dry in a very low oven or a warm cabinet, which can take 48 hours or longer. (See page 311 for more information on drying fruits.)

# Natural decoration variations

**Simple orange pomanders** Make natural baubles by evenly scoring orange skins and slowly dehydrating the fruits *(p.65)*.

**Fruit and flower sprigs** For simple, stylish decorations, tie stems of rosehips to dried teazle heads with wire and finish with a loop.

**Spiced fruits** Attach single fruits and dried sliced chiles with colored wire to either end of a decorated orange slice *(pp.64–65)*.

**Frosted Christmas lanterns** Use a few wispy seed heads instead of a thistle head to give this decoration *(pp.62–63)* a frosted effect.

**Citrus slices** Make a hole in the top of a dried orange slice, thread through a length of string, and secure in a knot.

**Cinnamon walnut bundles** Attach a walnut at either end of thin rope, wrap the rope around the sticks, and glue on a star anise.

**Cranberry hearts** Thread thin string through dried cranberries using a needle, secure in a heart shape, and finish with a loop.

**Snow clouds** Tie extra quantites of wispy or fluffy seed heads to Chinese lanterns with thin wire and finish with a loop.

# Fabric and paper Christmas tree

These delightful decorations are all made from eco-friendly materials, such as vintage fabric (pp.70–71, 78–79), old, woollen blankets (pp.72–73, 80–81), and discarded paper (pp.76–77), and are endlessly reusable, or recyclable.

# Doll pin tree angel

★ ★ ★  LEVEL OF DIFFICULTY

An old-fashioned peg doll has a nostalgic appeal that makes it a perfect decoration for any Christmas tree. If your tree is small, hang the angel right at the top of the tree, or for a larger tree make up several angels to dress the branches. Use a traditional wooden clothes peg to create the angel's body; if you can't buy any of these pegs locally, try finding them on the internet.

## materials

- Recycled natural raffia
- 1 doll pin
- Eco-friendly adhesive glue
- Eco-friendly marker pen
- Old tablecloth
- Templates *(pp.318-19)*
- Scissors
- Cotton thread and needle, or sewing machine
- Garden wire, about 6 in (15 cm) long
- Cream felt *(p.28)*
- Recycled ribbon

**1** Attach a few short strands of raffia to the top of the dolly peg with a dab of glue. Draw two eyes onto the peg head with the marker pen.

**2** Cut two shapes from the cloth using the template. Align and sew the sides of the dress together, leaving a gap in the neck to fit the peg.

**3** Twist one end of the wire into a circle. Bend the free end at right angles to the circle. Wind it around the peg to secure the halo in place.

**4** Cut the wings from the felt using the template. Glue a loop of ribbon, then the dress, onto the wings. Glue the peg inside the dress.

# A flock of festive birds

★ ★ ★   LEVEL OF DIFFICULTY

These beautiful felt tree decorations are fun to make and last a lifetime. The basic method is straightforward; it's up to you how sophisticated you want the decorations and details to be. Take your inspiration from your favorite birds, and make these felt birds as colorful as you like. Make them uniquely personal by adding a family member's initials to each finished decoration.

**1** Cut two body and wing shapes and some flower and leaf shapes for each bird. Make a hole in the top of each body shape with a skewer.

**2** Stitch a flower eye onto the outside of each body shape at the head, then sew some flower and leaf motifs onto the body and wings.

**3** Embroider simple patterns onto the felt shapes, then sew the two body shapes together using blanket stitch. Repeat with the two wing shapes.

**4** Cut a slit close to the top of the bird's body and push through the sewn wings. Thread the leather strip through the hole and tie it in a loop.

## materials

- Felt in assorted colors
- Festive bird templates (pp.320–21)
- Scissors
- Skewer
- Colored embroidery thread and needle
- Leather strips or lengths of twine
- Found and recycled materials to decorate the bird (optional, see tip)

### 🍃 Green tip

**Recycled decorations** Source a variety of items from the garden or kitchen shelves or drawers to decorate each bird. Look out for grasses, twigs, dried flowers, dried beans, rice and pasta, bay leaves, old candy wrappers, buttons, and vintage beads.

## Festive bird variations

Decorate these exquisite birds in flight with whatever foraged materials you can find: glue on a few grass heads, twigs, or thin ribbons to create plumage; or sew on some recycled sequins or vintage beads to make the birds sparkle as they catch the light.

# Recycled paper decorations

★ ★ ★    LEVEL OF DIFFICULTY

It's worth collecting all sorts of attractive or colorful recycled papers to make these child-friendly tree decorations. Look out for wallpaper samples, pages from magazines, and old oddments of wrapping paper, and recycle the cardboard from items such as tea and cereal boxes to use as the backing material for each decoration.

## materials

### For each decoration

- Template *(pp.322–25)*
- Recycled paper in festive colors
- Recycled cardboard
- Eco-friendly adhesive glue
- Scissors
- Length of string or wool
- 1 vintage bead or button

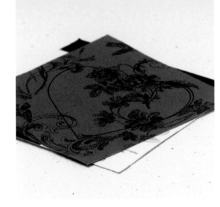

**1** Place the template on the piece of paper and draw around it. Cut out a piece of cardboard roughly the same size as the piece of paper.

**2** Glue the piece of recycled cardboard onto the back of the paper and leave to one side for a while for the glue to dry completely.

### 🍃 Green tip

**Eco decorations**
It's worth making your own tree decorations, as bought decorations are often chemically treated, or made from non-biodegradable substances.

**3** Cut out the paper shape neatly using a sharp pair of scissors. Trim the shape if necessary so that no pen or pencil marks are showing.

**4** Thread both ends of the string through a bead or button to create a loop. Glue the string loop to the back of the card and allow to dry.

# Scented fabric hearts

★ ★ ★  LEVEL OF DIFFICULTY

These pretty little filled fabric hearts look adorable hanging from a tree, but they can also be given as stocking stuffers to be hung in closets or tucked into drawers to fragrance clothes. Dried lavender flowers or natural potpourri both make ideal fillings, or fill the hearts with grains of dried rice or barley fragranced with a few drops of your favorite scented essential oil.

**1** Using the template, cut out two heart shapes from the fabric. Align and sew them together around the edges, leaving a small gap on one side.

**2** Snip gently around the edges of the seams with the scissors, taking care not to cut the stitching. Then turn the fabric inside out.

**3** Iron the fabric to get rid of any creases, then pack the heart with the scented filling. Sew up the open gap with the needle and thread.

**4** Make a knot at one end of the string and sew it onto the heart. Thread the string through the stick and leaves, knot it, and finish in a loop.

## materials

- Heart template (p.326)
- Recycled fabric (use an old gingham tea towel or tablecloth)
- Scissors or pinking shears
- Cotton thread and needle
- Your choice of filling, such as dried lavender
- Length of string
- 1 cinnamon stick with a hole through the center (use a knitting needle or skewer to do this)
- Several dried bay leaves with a hole through the center of each

# Fabric candy cane cones

★★☆ LEVEL OF DIFFICULTY

These cones look utterly irresistible when filled with sweet treats and hung from the tree. If you line the inside of each cone with a little baking parchment to protect the fabric from the sugary treats, you can use these decorations over and over again. For a more rustic effect, wrap the piece of wire around your finger and into a coil first before attaching it to the cone.

## materials

**For each decoration**

- A piece of cream felt (use an old felted blanket, *p.28*)
- Recycled fabric for lining
- Template *(p.327)*
- Scissors
- Pins
- Cotton thread and needle or sewing machine
- Knitting needle
- Colored embroidery thread for sewing around the rim of the cone
- A short length of recycled ribbon
- Vintage or recycled button
- Red wool (optional)
- A length of wire approximately 20 in (50 cm) long

**1** Cut one cone shape from the felt and one from the lining fabric. Align and pin the fabric shapes together, correct sides facing inwards.

**2** Stitch the short edges together. Fold lengthways, correct sides facing inwards. Stitch the curved edges together, leaving the lining half unsewn.

**3** Turn the fabric inside out through the gap in the lining using a knitting needle. Leave a band of lining showing at the top of the cone.

**4** Sew around the rim to hold the lining in place. Decorate with a ribbon and button, or sew on red wool spots. Attach the wire at either side.

# Edible Christmas tree

Tempt your family and friends with delicious homemade sweets (pp.88–89), cookies (pp.84–85, 236–37), and other edible treats (pp.310–11) hanging on your Christmas tree.

# Iced cookie decorations

★ ★ ★  LEVEL OF DIFFICULTY

This simple gingerbread recipe is easy to follow and makes about 35 edible tree decorations. The dough is easy to handle, so children will love rolling it, cutting out different festive shapes, and decorating the baked cookies with icing. Keep an eye on the cookies while they bake, as they may burn.

**1** Put the flour, baking soda, ginger, and cinnamon in a bowl. Rub in the butter so the mix resembles breadcrumbs. Stir in the sugar.

**2** Add the egg and syrup, then mix to form a dough. Turn out onto a lightly floured surface and knead to bring the dough together (p.226).

**3** Divide the dough into two batches. Roll each batch out with a lightly floured rolling pin to an even thickness of about ¼ in (5 mm).

**4** Cut shapes with cookie cutters, make a hole in each with a skewer, place on greased baking trays, and bake for about 10 minutes.

## ingredients

Preheat the oven to 375°F (190°C)

- 3 cups all-purpose flour
- 1 tsp baking soda
- 2 tsp ground ginger
- 2 tsp ground cinnamon
- 1 stick butter, cut into pieces
- ¾ cup light unrefined sugar
- 1 egg, beaten
- 4 tbsp sugar syrup

### For the icing
- 1 egg white, beaten with 5–7 oz (150–200 g) confectioner's sugar (adjust the quantity slightly, depending on the size of the egg; the icing should be smooth)

# Iced cookie variations

**Angel** Beat the egg white and confectioner's sugar until smooth consistency. Pipe patterns to suit shapes like this angel.

**Christmas tree** Add organic red coloring to a separate batch of icing to make these color-contrasting tree decorations.

**Heart** Pipe on these straight and fluted lines with a piping bag or a clean, recycled plastic sandwich bag with the corner cut off.

**Shooting star** Reopen any holes that close during baking, then pipe icing around them to make patterns like these star shapes.

**Holly leaf** Press the piping bag gently and evenly with both hands as you draw on intricate details like these holly leaf berries.

**Star** To create repeat patterns like this star shape, ice the outside edge first and echo the shape as you work inwards.

**Snowman** Change the piping bag nozzle to one with serrated edges for patterned details like the buttons on this snowman.

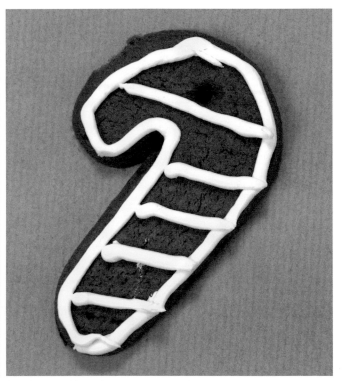

**Candy cane** Keep the patterns on slim-shaped cookies clear and simple, such as the outline and stripes on this candy cane.

# Nougat sweets

★ ★ ★   LEVEL OF DIFFICULTY

These wonderfully sticky, very light soft sweets are perfect for filling tiny galvanized buckets or fabric candy cane cones, hanging from the Christmas tree. You'll need a sugar thermometer to ensure that the sugar solution reaches the correct temperature as it boils; be aware that it is extremely hot at this stage, so don't let children come too close to the pan.

## ingredients

- 3½ cups granulated sugar
- 1½ cups sugar syrup
- ¼ cup clear honey
- 1 cup water
- 2 egg whites, beaten until stiff in a large bowl
- 1 tsp vanilla extract
- 10 oz (275 g) mixture of blanched almonds, hazelnuts, and macadamia nuts

**1** Heat the sugar, syrup, honey and water in a saucepan until it reaches 310°F (154°C). Stand the thermometer in the pan to check the temperature.

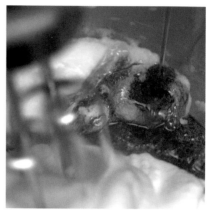

**2** When the sugar solution is ready, add it to the bowl of beaten egg whites, beating the mixture constantly until it is stiff and waxy.

**3** Add the vanilla extract and the nuts to the bowl and fold them all carefully into the mixture using a large metal spoon.

**4** Put the nougat mix into a tin lined with wax paper. Allow to cool completely before cutting it into small squares. Store in an airtight tin.

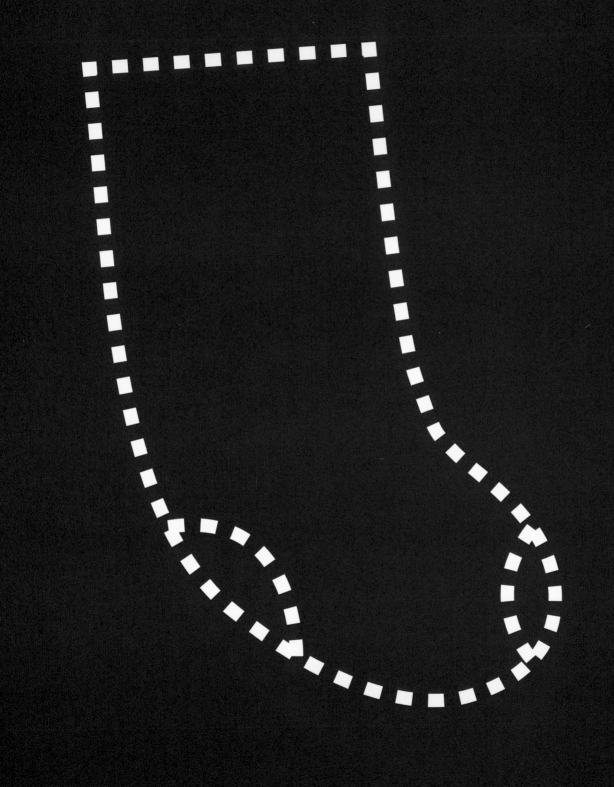

# GIVING

# Advent calendar sacks

★ ★ ★    LEVEL OF DIFFICULTY

If you want a change from the traditional, flat card Advent calendars, try making these fabric sacks to hang on your Christmas tree, or use them to decorate a smaller table-top tree. They are easy to make, and can be filled with whatever treats your family enjoys—try a mixture of home-made sweets, bite-size cookies, fresh nuts, and tiny gifts.

**1** Using the template, cut the cloth into 48 sack shapes. Then cut 24 small squares of fabric, each about 1¼ x 1¼ in (3 x 3 cm) in size.

**2** Align two sack shapes, correct sides facing inward. Sew three sides together. Leave a seam of ½ in (1 cm). Repeat with the other shapes.

**3** Mark a day of Advent, from 1 to 24, on each fabric square. Make a hole in the top corner of each square, thread through the twine, and knot it.

**4** Fill each sack with a few treats, then tie the twine around the top to seal the sack. Secure the ends in a loop and hang from the tree.

## materials

- Template *(p.328)*
- Old tablecloth, or pretty curtain material
- Scissors or pinking shears
- Cotton needle and thread or sewing machine
- Eco-friendly marker pen
- 24 lengths of garden twine or string, each about 12½ in (32 cm) long
- Treats to fill each sack

# Stocking Advent calendar

★ ★ ★   LEVEL OF DIFFICULTY

Add to the excitement of present-giving with this simple Advent calendar, which can be hung across a mantlepiece, along your stair banisters, or around a tree. Fill each stocking with a few of your family's favorite sweet treats, small edibles, or tiny gifts, attach fabric numbers to the stockings if you wish, and then mark the 24 days of Advent by opening each stocking in turn.

## materials

- An old, plain linen bed sheet, or two plain linen pillowcases
- An old gingham table cloth, or two large gingham tea towels
- Template (p.329)
- Scissors or pinking shears
- Pins
- Cotton thread and needle, or a sewing machine
- 24 short lengths of twine or string, each about 6 in (15 cm) long
- A long length of twine or string
- Fabric numbers (optional) (p.93)

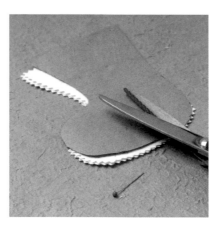

**1** Cut 24 shapes from the linen cloth using the template (secure it with a pin if necessary). Cut another 24 shapes from the gingham cloth.

**2** Align two shapes of the same fabric. Sew the edges, but not the top, together, correct sides facing out. Repeat with all the fabric shapes.

**3** Tie each short piece of string in a loop. Sew a loop onto the top right corner of each stocking. Sew on small bows made from the fabric.

**4** Tie the stockings, alternating the fabrics, into place along the long length of twine so they are evenly spaced. Add fabric numbers, if needed.

# Plant cuttings

★ ★ ★   LEVEL OF DIFFICULTY

Cuttings taken from your favourite plants and potted up as gifts in decorated pots will always be appreciated by family and friends—a beautifully scented rose or philadelphus shrub, or a harvest of sweet succulent redcurrants can provide years of enjoyment and pleasure. You may also like to think about starting a long-term project for a gift, such as growing oak saplings from acorns.

**1** Cut approximately 10 long stems from each selected plant, about 8–12 in (20–30 cm) in length. Cut just above a bud on the parent plant.

**2** Arrange in separate piles and select the healthiest-looking stems. Remove the top 2 in (5 cm) of softer growth at the tips of the stem.

**3** Cut each stem into 3 or 4 at an angle to enhance growth. Trim the base of the cutting just below a bud, and the top just above a bud.

**4** Plant the 3 cuttings in one pot in case any fail to thrive. Fill the pot base with a few crocks, add compost, insert the cuttings, and add a tag.

## materials

- Selection of shrubs. For example, rose, redcurrant, gooseberry, blackcurrant, and philadelphus
- Garden shears
- Some broken pottery or pebbles
- Organic, peat-free, multi-purpose compost
- Selection of pots (terracotta, wicker, and coconut matting are all suitable)
- Pot tags labeled with the name of the plant, and with instructions to plant the cuttings after Christmas, then dig up the established seedlings the following winter and replant them separately

# Plant a herb basket

Make the perfect Christmas gift for a food lover by choosing a small selection of fresh herbs such as parsley, rosemary, thyme, and purple sage, and planting them in an attractive basket *(p.99)*.

## Savory Christmas basket

A basket filled with homemade chutney (pp.134–35), pickled shallots, flavored oil (pp.124–25), a bag of sweet chestnuts, and a cooked ham wrapped in wax paper (pp.268–69) makes a delightful gift (p.190).

# Christmas stocking

★ ★ ★   LEVEL OF DIFFICULTY

Stockings are a great way of giving gifts without having to wrap each item. They are also useful for decorating the home; if you hang them up early, they will add to the excitement of Christmas approaching. You can customize each stocking by sewing on a decorative bow, an individual's initials, or fabric shapes on a favorite theme, or wind a piece of trailing ivy around the top of the stocking.

## materials

- Embroidered tablecloth or an unwanted curtain
- Template *(pp.330-31)*
- Scissors
- Extra fabric to decorate
- Cotton thread and needle, or a sewing machine
- A piece of fabric 1 x 5 in (2.5 x 12 cm) for the loop

### 🌿 Green tip

**Using recycled fabric**
If someone has a much-loved garment that is no longer fit to wear, use it as the fabric for their stocking. If the material is very worn, sew it onto a piece of plain cotton or burlap material first, and then cut out the stocking shape.

**1** Cut out two stocking shapes using the template. Sew on any fabric details, such as a length of fabric, around the width of the stocking.

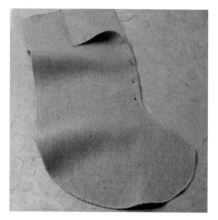

**2** Align the shapes, correct sides facing inward, and sew together, leaving a seam of ½in (1.5 cm) around the edge. Leave the top unstitched.

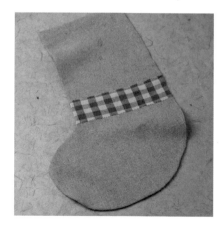

**3** Fold over and sew the fabric at the top of the stocking so the edges don't show. Then turn the stocking the right way round.

**4** Fold the fabric into a loop and sew it to the top of the stocking. Sew on more decorations as you wish. Make more stockings in the same way.

# Seaside foot scrub

★ ★ ★   LEVEL OF DIFFICULTY

This natural foot scrub is wonderful for sloughing off dead skin during the winter months—it's as good for your feet as walking barefoot along a sandy beach. Try beachcombing for a small scallop shell or another attractive shell to package up with the jar as a scoop, or ask at your local fish store for any spare scallop shells.

**1** Put all the dry ingredients into the preserving jar and mix them together with the spatula or spoon.

**2** Gradually add the olive oil and stir the ingredients well with the spatula as you pour.

**3** Add six drops of peppermint essential oil or foot gel, if you wish. The peppermint gives the scrub an extra freshness.

**4** Give the ingredients a last stir, seal the jar, add the label, and tie on the shell with the ribbon or raffia.

## materials

- 1 cup sand
- 1 tbsp sea salt
- 1 tbsp powdered dulse seaweed (available from health-food stores)
- 1 tbsp powdered kelp
- 1 wide-necked preserving jar, or kilner jar, with an airtight, hinged lid
- Wooden spatula or spoon
- 7fl oz (200 ml) olive oil
- Peppermint foot gel or essential oil (optional)
- 1 label listing the name of the scrub, and with instructions to apply a little of the scrub to the soles of the feet in a circular rubbing motion, paying particular attention to any hard areas of skin
- 1 scallop shell
- Recycled ribbon or natural raffia

# Decorated photo album

★ ★ ★   LEVEL OF DIFFICULTY

Although this decorated cover will always be delicate, it turns an ordinary-looking album into a beautiful, personalized gift. Choose a photo album or a large notebook with a neutral cloth or cardboard cover and good-quality, thick paper. Gather leaves as they start to turn rich, fall colors and look for interesting seed heads, grasses, and other natural materials.

## materials

- 1 photo album
- Variety of natural materials dried flat *(p.16)*
- Eco-friendly adhesive glue

### 🍃 Green tip

**Save tissue paper**
Reserve any sheets of tissue paper that are wrapped around goods you buy or receive and, using an iron on a low setting, iron out the creases. Use the tissue paper to cover and protect delicate items like this album cover when not in use.

**1** When your natural materials are all flattened and thoroughly dried, glue a row of seed heads or leaves along the top of the front cover.

**2** For each subsequent row, glue on materials that are roughly the same size in a pattern. Overlap or alternate some materials.

**3** Continue to build up the pattern by gluing on rows of colored leaves, grasses, and twigs until the front cover is completely filled up.

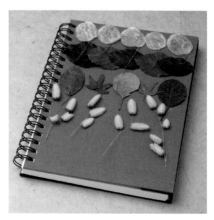

**4** Leave the glued materials to dry, then cover the book carefully in several layers of tissue paper before gift-wrapping it in a recycled box.

# Give eco gifts

Choose gifts that make a positive difference to the environment, or people in need (donate a charitable gift to buy a life-saving piece of equipment, such as a mosquito net, for example). Buy items from your local shops or on the internet, and to be even more eco-friendly, choose gifts that don't need to be wrapped.

## Home–workers

### Staple-less stapler
This gadget punches two holes through sheets of paper and creates paper tabs that lock the papers together.

### Recycled notebooks and stationery
Choose paper products that have been produced from 100 percent recycled paper.

### Natural desk light
The high-efficiency natural spectrum flourescent bulb in this desk lamp imitates natural daylight, helping to reduce glare and eyestrain. The bulb lasts five times longer than an ordinary effervescent bulb.

### Intelliplug
Choose an energy-saving adapter plug for all computer and television equipment.

## Food lovers

### Organic fruit and vegetable box
Pay for a month's supply of home-delivered, fresh, locally grown produce.

### Indoor winter herb garden
Provide an attractive container or windowbox, some packets of herb seeds, and potting compost for a constant supply of fresh herbs.

## Homeowners

### Bath towels and bathrobes
Buy fairly traded, organic cotton bath towels and bathrobes, or choose organic cotton and bamboo fiber towels, which have a 30 percent higher absorbency than cotton-only towels.

### Furniture-making class
Select a class that teaches students how to make chairs and baskets from elm and willow, or to reupholster old furniture.

### Recycled glass homeware
Buy wineglasses, jugs, decanters, and bowls in stylish colors and designs.

### Eco kettle
This kettle boils only the amount of water you actually need, saving water, energy and time.

### Bamboo serving bowls
Choose streamlined, chic tableware made from bamboo—one of nature's greatest renewable sources. Fewer pesticides and chemical fertilizers are used on bamboo because it grows so fast.

# Babies and children

### Cloth diaper starter kit
Reusable cloth diapers are easy to use and wash, and avoid potentially harmful super-absorbent gels, deodorants and chemicals.

### Organic cotton clothes
Clothes made from organic cotton cause less harm to the environment, and to children's skin.

### Natural toys
Avoid plastic and PVC toys, which can contain harmful toxins, and choose toys made from natural wood, cotton, and wool.

# Adventurers

### Recycled wool travel picnic blanket
Look for rugs made from 100 percent pre- and post-consumer recycled wool.

### Wind-up gadgets
Choose a wind-up radio, or a media player for music, movie clips, and photos. One minute of winding gives one hour of radio listening or 40 minutes of media-playing time.

### Recycled backpack
Buy a backpack that is made from 98 percent recycled PET plastic bottles.

# Gardeners

### Tree
Give a "Grow-a-tree" kit, or have a couple of fruiting trees delivered by a local nursery.

### Water butt
Invaluable for collecting and storing rainwater to water plants in dry weather, it also reduces water consumption and water bills.

### Butterfly feeding station
Buy a nectar feeder to attract and feed butterflies and early-pollinating bees, and include a book on butterflies as part of the kit.

### Cold frame
A perfect gift for a gardener to raise seedlings and cuttings, or over-winter young plants.

### No-dig potato planter
This tough, woven, polyethylene planter with drainage holes holds about 9 gallons (40 liters) of compost in which to grow potatoes.

# Sports fans

### Sports shares
Contributing to a local sports association can entitle a shareholder to a certificate, club information, and an invitation to games.

### Fair-trade sporting goods
Balls and other gear made by a fair-trade agreement ensures that the workers have better wages and improved working conditions.

### Eco mat
A Synergy eco mat for yoga and Pilates is free of latex, PVC, and phlates, which all contain potentially harmful toxins.

### Eco surfboard
Many modern surfboards are toxic pieces of sports equipment; give an eco-friendly surfboard made of wood and and plant-based resin instead.

# Fabric notebook

★ ★ ★   LEVEL OF DIFFICULTY

A brightly colored, cheery-looking notebook is always a welcome and useful gift, and if you have made it yourself it will be even more appreciated. An easy approach is to buy a ready-bound notebook and decorate the cover, but stitching and binding the paper folios together and then covering them is quite straightforward once you get the hang of it.

**1** Align the 12 folios, with folds on the same side. Pierce 6 evenly spaced holes in each folio with a pin, then sew the folios together with running stitch.

**2** Cut the piece of muslin cloth so that it is the same length and width as the joined folios. Then glue it over the stitched folio folds.

**3** Glue the rectangles (the thinnest in the middle) to the fabric with a slight gap between. Glue down the fabric edges. Glue the page half over the cover.

**4** Glue half of each folded paper to an inside cover and, after glueing the muslin strip to the spine, glue the other half to an outer folio paper.

## materials

- Approximately 60 sheets of letter-sized, undyed, recycled paper divided into 12 piles of 5 sheets of paper: each pile is then folded in half to make a "folio"
- Linen thread and darning needle
- Strip of muslin cloth
- Eco-friendly adhesive glue
- 2 rectangles of recycled cardboard cut to the same size as the folded folios, and 1 rectangle cut the same size as the muslin cloth
- Old, pretty recycled fabric cut just slightly larger than an sheet of paper
- 1 illustrated page from an old, unwanted book
- 2 sheets of brightly colored recycled letter-sized paper, each folded in half

# Shrunken wool pots

★ ★ ★   LEVEL OF DIFFICULTY

If you've accidentally shrunken a favorite woollen garment in the wash, this is the perfect way to recycle it and turn it into a quirky, functional gift. These holders can be used to store anything from stationery to sewing kits, make-up, or cufflinks. Encourage good habits by filling some of the holders with recycled stationery as part of the gift.

## materials

- An old, shrunken, 100 percent wool garment or scarf, or thick sheets of felt *(p.28)*
- Pins
- Scissors
- Embroidery thread and needle
- Scraps of felt cut into 1 in (3 cm) squares

**1** Draw and cut out a template that has a base and four equal sides. Attach it with pins to the piece of felt and draw around it.

**2** Cut out the fabric shape with a pair of scissors. Press the fabric or starch it to flatten the base and sides as much as possible.

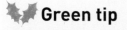 **Green tip**

**Eco-friendly stationery**
As well as recycled paper and envelopes, you can now buy eco-friendly, recycled, and biodegradable pens, marker pens, and pencils. When buying sustainable wooden pencils, look for the FSC (Forest Stewardship Council) logo.

**3** Sew the edges of the four sides together with a needle and thread using cross stitch. Put to one side while you make the felt flowers.

**4** Pinch each square into a flower shape. Sew the edges together at the center, leaving a length of thread at the back to attach to the holder.

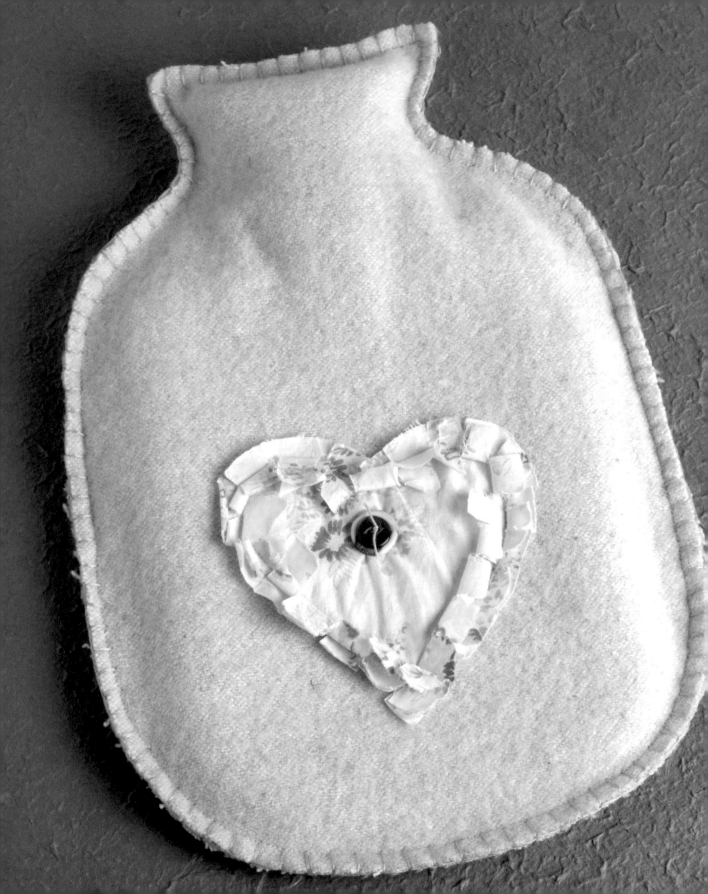

# Hot-water bottle cover

★ ★ ★  LEVEL OF DIFFICULTY

This lovely winter gift is quite simple to make and will delight anyone who receives it. Collect scraps of pretty cotton material, or look in secondhand and charity shops for natural fabrics with vintage patterns and colors to make the details on this cover really unique. If you don't have an old blanket to use for the cover, use any thick, recycled soft fabric.

## materials

- Template (pp.332–34)
- Woollen blanket or similar thick material
- Scissors
- 2 heart or star shapes, cut from scraps of fabric to decorate the front of the cover. Alternatively, cut 2 long strips of fabric
- Pins
- Cotton thread and needle or sewing machine
- Colored embroidery thread and needle for blanket stitch
- 2 recycled or vintage buttons

**1** Using the template, cut a front panel and two back half-panels. Pin decorative shapes to the front of the cover.

**2** Sew the fabric shapes onto the front panel, leaving a seam ½in (1 cm) wide. Snip the fabric edges every ½in (1 cm) to make a ruffle.

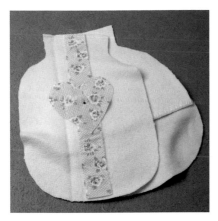

**3** Sew the buttons onto the fabric shape. Sew the panels together, leaving a seam of ¼in (6 mm). The back panels should overlap slightly.

**4** Using the colored embroidery thread and needle, sew all the way round the edges of the cover using blanket stitch.

# Natural Christmas cards

★ ★ ★    LEVEL OF DIFFICULTY

If you want to post any of these homemade three-dimensional cards, choose those with the least delicate, flattest decorations and cut a piece of recycled cardboard the same size as the card. Cover the front of the decorated card with the cardboard before sealing it in an envelope. This should, hopefully, protect the decorations from disintegrating or breaking in transit.

## materials

- Recycled card
- Scissors
- Scalpel
- Ruler
- Found objects such as seed heads, twigs and leaves in different sizes, dried flat *(p.16)*
- Spices such as star anise and cinnamon sticks
- Dried ingredients such as orange slices *(p.65)* and bay leaves
- Eco-friendly adhesive glue

**1** Cut a piece of recycled cardboard to the correct size. Score lightly down the middle of the card in a straight line using a scalpel and ruler.

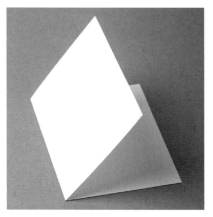

**2** Fold the card in half along the scored line, which will ensure a clean fold down the center of the card.

**3** Arrange and stick a dried leaf onto the front of the card using small dabs of glue.

**4** Glue two smaller leaves onto the larger leaf and attach one star anise at the base of the leaves. Then leave to one side to dry completely.

# Make flavored oils

Homemade infused oils are a wonderfully instant way of adding an extra shot of flavor to your cooking, salads, and marinades. They make a perfect gift for food lovers and serious cooks alike, so bottle a selection of flavored oils and add gift labels, or include one or two in a gift hamper. Good flavorings to use include fresh herbs, garlic, whole spices, pink peppercorns, or dried chiles.

Infused oils have the potential to support the growth of bacteria, so you should follow the procedures for bottling flavored oils carefully, and make sure that any ingredients you use are washed and thoroughly dried first. Use pretty recycled bottles or jars for these oils.

## Sterilizing equipment

It's important to sterilize all bottles or jars and their lids before adding any ingredients. Wash them in soapy water, or put them through a hot dishwasher wash, and leave to drain until nearly dry. Then place them upside down in a cold oven and heat them for 10—15 minutes at 300°F (150°C). Leave them upturned on a clean cloth until you are ready to use them so that dust or dirt, which could contaminate the product, can't be trapped inside. Alternatively, you can boil the bottles in a large saucepan covered with water for 15 minutes, dry them thoroughly with a fresh clean cloth, and upturn them onto another cloth until they are ready to be used.

## Making the oils

Make the flavored oil a week before you want to give it as a gift. For Rosemary oil, choose 1 large sprig of fresh rosemary (about 6in /15 cm long) and bruise it with the end of a rolling pin; for Lemon oil use 3–4 large ribbons of lemon peel; for Chile oil use 3–4 whole chiles cut in half lengthways. Put your choice of dry ingredients into a clear, sterilized glass bottle (at least 1 pint/570 ml in capacity) and add 1 pint (570 ml) of light olive oil. Make sure the dry ingredients stay below the surface of the oil, or they may turn mouldy. Secure the lid firmly and shake well once a day for a week to allow the flavors to develop. Add a gift label with instructions to store the oil in the fridge and use within a week.

Wash and thoroughly dry all ingredients to be used as flavorings before putting them in a bottle and adding the oil.

# Chocolate brownies

★ ★ ★   LEVEL OF DIFFICULTY

Once packaged in an airtight tin, these irresistable chocolate brownies will stay their best for up to six days. Don't overcook them or they will lose their soft, fudgy quality; look for a dull crust to form, then quickly take them out of the oven. You can make the brownies in advance, freeze them, and leave them to thaw in a tin—there will be no excess moisture.

## ingredients

Preheat the oven to 375°F (190°C)

- 12 oz (350 g) bittersweet chocolate, broken into small pieces
- 8 oz (225 g) butter, cut into small cubes
- 2 tsp instant coffee granules
- 2 tbsp hot water
- 4 eggs
- 8 oz (225 g) superfine sugar
- 1 tsp vanilla extract
- 3 oz (75 g) self-rising flour
- 8 oz (225 g) bittersweet chocolate chips or small chunks of bittersweet chocolate

**1** Grease and line a 12 x 9 in (30 x 23 cm) baking tray with parchment paper. Put chocolate pieces and butter cubes in a bowl.

**2** Melt the chocolate and butter slowly in a double boiler: rest the bowl over a pan of gently simmering water on a low heat.

**3** Dissolve the coffee granules in the water in a large bowl. Beat in the eggs, sugar, and vanilla extract. Then beat in the chocolate mixture.

**4** Fold in the flour and chocolate chips. Pour the mix into the tray. Bake for 20–25 minutes, or until firm to the touch. Cut into squares once cool.

# Willow wigwam

★★☆ LEVEL OF DIFFICULTY

A willow wigwam covered in delicately scented climbing sweet peas always looks stunning in a mid-summer border. Christmas is the ideal moment to give a wigwam as a gift, and any gardener will appreciate this perfect timing as they make their preparations for what to plant, and where, in the following year. Buy your hazel rods and willow stems from sustainable sources.

**1** Upturn the flowerpot and gently push the base of each hazel rod into the grass around the pot. Space out the rods evenly in a circle.

**2** Gather the rods at the top and bind them together temporarily with twine. Trim the tops of the rods with shears to give a uniform height.

**3** Weave lengths of willow around the rods: pull each stem up and round as you weave it in and out. Weave 3 or 4 willow sections up the frame.

**4** Cut off the twine and wind some willow lengths around the top. Secure the ends by jamming them between the joined rods.

## materials

- 1 flowerpot or bucket (the size depends on how large you want the wigwam to be; a medium-sized flowerpot is ideal). Alternatively, use a large, earth-filled flowerpot or bucket and push the hazel rods in around the edge of the inside rim
- 5 or so straight hazel rods, a maximum of 7–8 ft (2.2–2.5 m) in length, each with a diagonal cut at the base
- Garden twine
- 10 or so long lengths of willow, each about ½ in (1 cm) thick
- Garden shears

# Fruit jam

★ ★ ★  LEVEL OF DIFFICULTY

It's worth making preserves and jams when you harvest your own fruit or buy it in season, but you can freeze fresh fruits like blackcurrants, raspberries, strawberries and cranberries, to make extra quantities of jam during the winter months. They'll make welcome gifts if you decorate the lids with pretty fabric and add a gift label. They are also a perfect addition to a Christmas gift basket.

## ingredients

- 4 lb (1.8 kg) fruit, washed and destalked
- 7½ cups water
- 6 lb (2.7 kg) sugar
- A pat of butter
- 10–12 jam jars

**To sterilize jars and lids**

Wash in soapy water or a hot dishwasher cycle. Drain until nearly dry. Place upside down in a cold oven. Heat for 10–15 minutes at 300°F (150°C). Keep upturned on a clean cloth until ready to use so dust or dirt can't contaminate the produce.

**To test for setting point**

Spoon a little boiling jam onto a plate and leave in the fridge to cool. It is set if it forms a skin that wrinkles when you push it with your fingertip. If it is still fluid, boil the jam a little longer and re-test.

**1** Defrost the fruits in a preserving pan or large, heavy-based pan. Add the water, bring to the boil, and simmer gently for about 45 minutes.

**2** Remove the pan from the heat, add the sugar to the fruit pulp, stir until dissolved, and add the butter. Then boil rapidly for 10–15 minutes.

**3** Sterilize the jam jars and lids *(left)*. Keep an eye on the boiling jam and stir it occasionally so that it doesn't catch on the base and burn.

**4** Test for a set every five minutes. When setting point is reached, leave to stand for 15 minutes, then pot up the jam and seal with airtight lids.

# Pear chutney

★ ★ ★   LEVEL OF DIFFICULTY

Use the largest heavy-based saucepan you have, or a preserving pan, to make chutney. As the ingredients simmer, check on them frequently and give them a stir so that they don't catch on the bottom of the pan and burn, which spoils the flavor. Then pot up the chutney in jars with vinegar-proof lids. To get a good spicy–sweet balance, leave the chutney to mature for at least three months.

**1** Put all the fruit and vegetables in the pan with no added liquid and simmer gently, uncovered, until tender, stirring occasionally.

**2** Wrap the peppercorns in the cheesecloth. Tie with the string to make a sachet. Then add it and the remaining ingredients to the pan.

**3** Simmer the chutney, uncovered, and stir often until it thickens and takes on a dark caramel color. This will take two to three hours.

**4** Remove the peppercorn sachet, put up the chutney in warm, sterilized jars *(p.132)*, and seal. Store in a cool, dark place.

## ingredients

**Makes c. 6 lb (2.5 kg)**

- 3 lb (1.4 kg) pears, peeled, cored and cut into ¾ in (2 cm) cubes
- 1 lb (450 g) onions, chopped
- 1 lb (450 g) green or red tomatoes, sliced
- 8 oz (250 g) raisins, chopped
- 6 peppercorns
- Small piece of cheesecloth
- Length of string
- 700 g (1½ lb) brown sugar
- 1 tsp cayenne pepper
- 1 tsp ground ginger
- 2 tsp salt
- 3 cups (750 ml) malt vinegar

# Recycled paper cards

★★☆ LEVEL OF DIFFICULTY

These cards are easy to make, and are a fun, child-friendly project. Tear out pages from old magazines with interesting patterns, illustrations, and festive photographs, or recycle wrapping paper, wallpaper samples, or the pictures from last year's Christmas cards. Use a selection of templates from the back of the book to cut out different shapes, or download some from the internet.

## materials

- Template *(pp.322–25)*
- Recycled pictures
- Scissors
- Plain, recycled cardboard (or find ready-made, plain recycled cards)
- Scalpel
- Ruler
- Eco-friendly adhesive glue

### Green tip

**Recycle your old cards**
Converting timber into paper is a very energy-intensive process, but recycling conserves resources and saves energy. Recycling all cards after Christmas in will save tens of thousands of tons of greenhouse gases each year.

**1** Draw a template of your choice and cut it out. If you are using a star template, make up the smallest star template as well.

**2** Place the template on a piece of illustrated or patterned recycled paper. Draw around the template and cut out the shape.

**3** Lightly score down the middle of the recycled card with a scalpel and ruler. Fold the card in half and glue the star shape onto the front.

**4** Using the smallest star template, cut tiny stars from the recycled paper and glue them onto the card around the main star. Allow to dry.

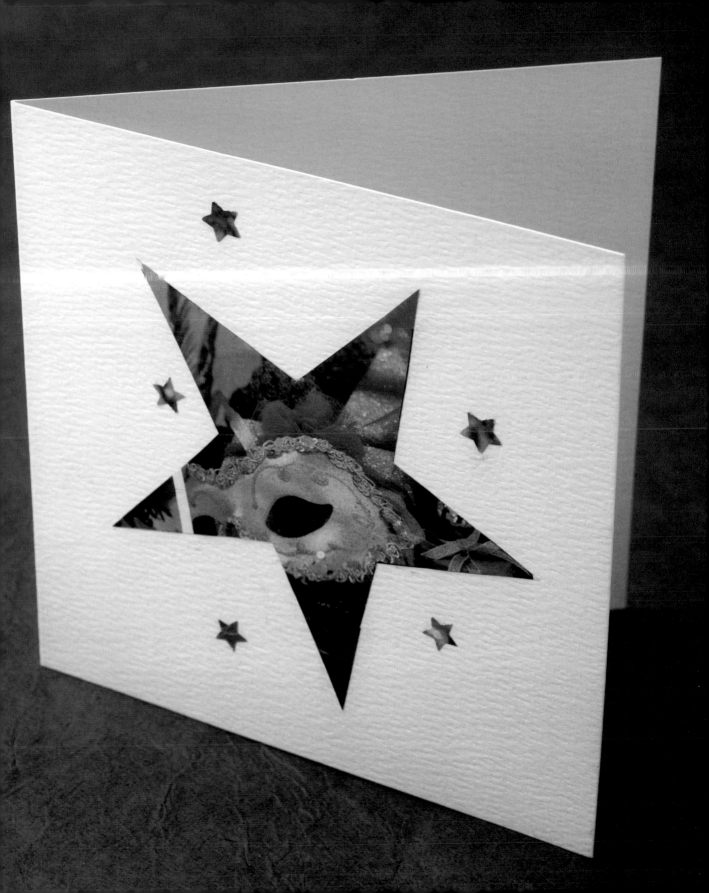

## Recycled paper card variations

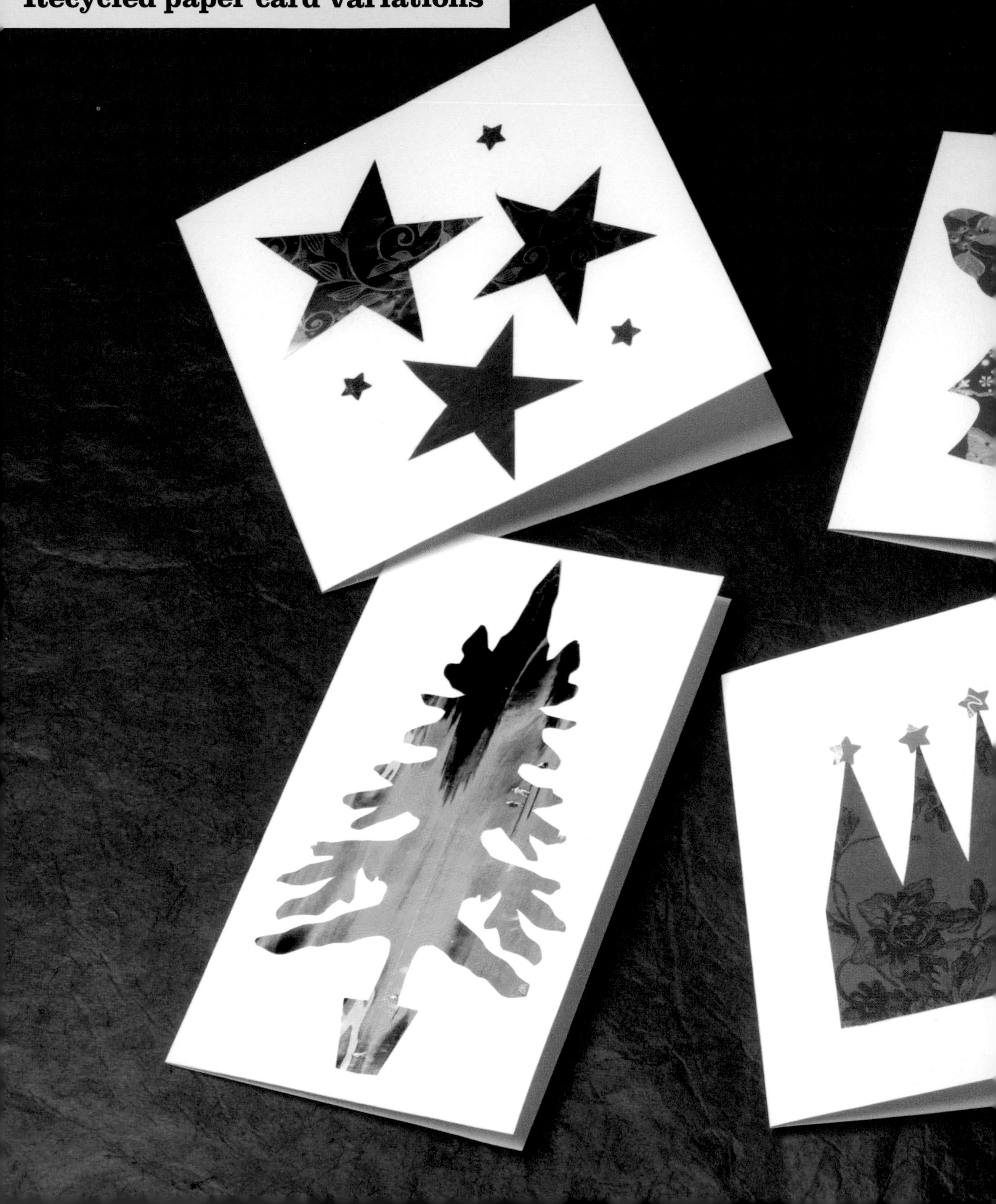

# Herbal tea sachets

★ ★ ★   LEVEL OF DIFFICULTY

If you grow your own herbs, you may enjoy the fresh leaves or flowers in tisanes, but it's easy to dry them and make them into herbal tea sachets to give as gifts. Dried herbs are more concentrated in taste, since they contain no moisture, so you'll need fewer dried herbs than you would fresh. Store the dried herbs separately in jars until you make the sachets, to retain their individual flavor.

**1** Tip the dried herb of your choice out of its storage jar and gently crumble the leaves or flower heads.

**2** Arrange two teaspoons of the dried herb in the middle of one of the cheesecloth squares.

**3** Gather the edges of the cloth square into the center, wrap the piece of twine around the top of the sachet, and secure firmly in a bow.

**4** Leave the ends of the twine long so that the used sachet can be lifted out of a teacup. Make five more sachets, then gift-wrap them in the box.

## materials

- 6 squares cheesecloth measuring 7 x 7 in (18 x 18 cm)
- 12 tsp dried herbs
- 6 pieces of twine or recycled string
- Recycled cardboard box lined with layers of recycled tissue paper and a remnant of fabric

### 🍂 Green tip

**Drying fresh herbs**
Staple some cheesecloth to a wooden frame. Lay leaves and flower heads on the cloth. Leave in a warm, dry, well-ventilated dark room and turn several times during the first week. The herbs are dry when they are crisp enough to crumble.

## Sweet Christmas basket

Give a variety of sweet, homemade produce as a gift: package up
chocolate brownies *(pp.126–27)*, a ginger cake *(pp.290–91)*, nougat
*(pp.88–89)*, and fruit jam *(pp.132–33)* in airtight tins, pretty boxes,
and decorated jars, and arrange them in a medium-sized basket.

# Sew a glove purse

★ ★ ☆  LEVEL OF DIFFICULTY

Turn any odd, or old, unwanted woollen mittens or gloves into these fun glove purses for children. Depending on the color of the glove, you could make a white snowman, a brown reindeer, or a red Santa Claus bag—or fill the inside of the glove with some stuffing, sew up the cuff, add button features, and attach a metal keyring hoop to turn it into a monster key ring.

## materials

- Unwanted or odd gloves
- Cotton thread and needle or sewing machine (optional)
- Scissors
- Small zip
- Pins
- Recycled buttons or beads
- Odd scraps of felt, wool, ribbon, or fabric

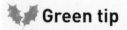 **Green tip**

**Recycle old clothes**
Many thousands of tons of old clothes are thrown away at Christmas each year. Donate good-quality clothes to charity shops or bins at recycling centers, and give the rest to clothing banks to be turned into rags for engineering industries.

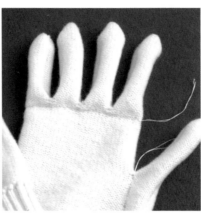

**1** Turn the glove inside out and sew along the bottom of each finger and the thumb (retain the forefinger and little finger if you want to create ears).

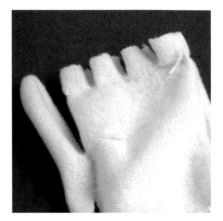

**2** Cut off each unwanted finger and the thumb with a pair of scissors about ¼ in (5 mm) away from the seam.

**3** Turn the glove the correct way around, then pin and sew the zipper into the rim of the cuff. Sew on buttons or beads for facial features.

**4** Use one cut-off finger to make a nose and sew it on, sew on buttons for eyes, then use felt or plaited lengths of wool as decoration.

# Fabric Christmas cards

★ ★ ★   LEVEL OF DIFFICULTY

These attractive cards can be easily adapted: use a loop of ribbon instead of string, or punch two small holes close together near the top of the card, thread through wool or twine, and tie it in a bow; or cut out and sew together two fabric shapes and fill the center with sweet-smelling dried lavender. Don't cut the shapes too small, or you may find them hard to sew and turn inside out.

**1** Make up your chosen template, then place it on a piece of fabric and cut around the shape neatly with a pair of scissors.

**2** Thread the string through the button or bead and secure the ends of the string in a knot.

**3** Glue the knotted end of the string loop onto the back of the fabric shape and allow to dry.

**4** Lightly score down the middle of the cardboard with a scalpel and ruler. Glue the fabric shape onto the front of the card. Allow to dry.

## materials

- Template *(pp.322-25)*
- Scraps of fabric, or old carpet samples, for an interesting texture
- Scissors
- Recycled string
- Recycled or vintage button or bead
- Eco-friendly adhesive glue
- Recycled cardboard
- Scalpel
- Ruler

# Dried herb sachets

★ ★ ★  LEVEL OF DIFFICULTY

Fill these pretty bags with whichever aromatic dried herbs and flowers you can find or have grown. Classic, popular choices are the leaves or flower heads from rosemary, pine, or lavender plants. You may also want to include some instructions to how to refresh the scent: either gently squeeze the contents of the bag occasionally, or add a couple of drops of lavender essential oil.

## materials

**For each herb sachet**
- Odd scraps of fabric, cut into squares or rectangles to make a piece of fabric 7 x 10 in (18 x 25 cm) large, or a piece of velvet, vintage ticking, linen, or similar material
- Pins
- Cotton thread and needle or sewing machine
- Template *(pp.338–39)*
- Scissors or pinking shears
- Recycled or vintage buttons and beads
- Scented filling
- Garden twine, string or recycled ribbon

**1** To make a piece of patchwork from the scraps of fabric, place them face down on a flat surface and arrange them into a pattern.

**2** Pin and sew the scraps together. Place the template on the patchwork material, or other fabric and cut out two bag shapes.

**3** Align the shapes, correct sides facing inward. Sew along three sides. Fold over and sew the raw edges at the top. Turn the right way around.

**4** Sew on buttons and beads to embellish the fabric. Pour the scented filling into the sachet and tie up the opening with twine or ribbon.

# Glossy lip balm

★ ★ ★  LEVEL OF DIFFICULTY

This organic lip balm gives lips a pretty sheen, and its rich butters and oils nourish the skin and prevent drying: petrochemical-based balms actually dry lips out over time, whereas this balm soothes and gradually smooths away dryness. Package the lip balm in a pretty box lined with recycled tissue paper and tied with a vintage ribbon or some natural raffia.

**1** Put the cocoa butter, coconut oil, almond oil, and beeswax in a heatproof bowl and melt them together in a double boiler (p.126).

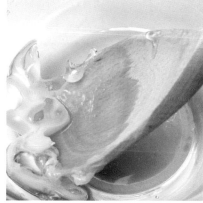

**2** Remove from the heat. Add the gel and your choice of essential oil (peppermint is invigorating and zingy; orange is aromatic and delectable).

**3** Mix the ingredients together using the whisk. The ingredients will cool quite quickly as you whisk, and turn an opaque color.

**4** Decant the mixture into the sterilized jar with a clean, dry teaspoon, and seal. Then package up the lip balm.

## materials

- 1 tsp cocoa butter, grated
- ½ tsp coconut oil
- 1 tsp sweet almond oil
- ½ tsp beeswax
- 1 tsp aloe vera gel
- 2 drops of sweet orange or peppermint essential oil
- 1 small whisk
- 1 small recycled eye cream or lip balm jar and lid, sterilized (p.125)

### 🍃 Green tip

**Use organic products**
Not all chemicals are bad for us, but harsh industrial chemicals in non-organic face and body products are. Use organic products or read ingredients labels and avoid parabens, fragrance (parfum), and detergents such as sodium lauryl sulfate.

# Moth-repellent sachets

★ ★ ★   LEVEL OF DIFFICULTY

Sachets filled with aromatic herbs make useful and attractive gifts. Moths dislike the strong smell of lavender and herbs such as rosemary, southernwood, tansy, and woodruff, so use a combination of these dried plants for the filling. Use any recycled material to make the sachets, but if you have a favorite old woollen sweater you can no longer wear, shrink it and use the soft, felted fabric.

## materials

- Shrunken, 100 percent wool garment *(p.28)*, or oddments of fabric
- Scissors
- Template *(pp.338-39)*; reduce the size of the template if you want to make more sachets
- Pins
- Cotton thread and needle, or sewing machine
- Recycled ribbon and buttons
- Filling of dried lavender *(Lavandula)* and strong-smelling herbs such as rosemary *(Rosemarinus)*, southernwood *(Artemisia abrotanum)*, tansy *(Tanacetum vulgare)* and woodruff *(Galium odoratum)*

**1** Cut down one side of the garment and open it out flat, correct side facing down. If you use the sleeves, cut them off and turn them inside out.

**2** Pin the template in place and cut out two rectangular shapes. Then align and pin the shapes together, correct sides facing inward.

**3** Sew around the edges, leaving a small seam and leaving the top or the cuff unsewn. Then turn the sachet the right way around.

**4** Cut some small hearts from the spare fabric. Sew them and a button onto the sachet or a ribbon, fill the sachet, and secure with the ribbon.

# Make flavored alcohol

If you gather blackberries from hedgerows in the fall, or if you have a bountiful harvest of raspberries or other fruits, turn some of the crop into fruity flavored alcoholic drinks. Use gin or vodka with the highest proof content to get the best preserving results. These wonderfully warming drinks take three and a half months to mature, and then continue to improve in flavor.

Alcohol is a preservative—nothing can grow in pure alcohol—and when fruits are soaked in it, the alcohol absorbs their flavor to give a fruity taste and color. Use ripe produce for the best quality and flavor and freeze the fruits until needed. Frozen fruit provides excellent results: the freezing process ruptures the fruit skins and allows the juices to flow out.

## To make Raspberry gin

To make about 1 quart (c. 1 liter):

- 1 bottle of gin (1¼ pints/700 ml)
- 2 cups raspberries, fresh or frozen
- 1 cup superfine sugar
- A few cloves (optional)
- 1 stick of cinnamon (optional)
- A few drops of almond extract (optional)
- 1 large, wide-necked jar, sterilized, or 2 empty gin bottles

Pour the gin, fruit, sugar, spices, and almond extract into the sterilized jar *(p.125)*, or divide the ingredients equally between two bottles using a funnel (there's no need to sterilize a vodka or gin bottle if the alcohol has just been poured out of it). Seal and store in a cool, dark place. Give the jar or bottles a shake daily for the first two weeks and then weekly for a further three months. During this

time the sugar dissolves and the liquor takes on a luscious red color. Take a sip every now and then and add more sugar if needed. After three and half months, or when the taste is to your liking, strain the ingredients, and re-bottle the liquid only.

To make **Sloe gin**, replace the raspberries with sloes and prick each sloe berry with a skewer before adding to the gin. To make **Blackberry** or **Damson** (Italian plum) **vodka**, replace the gin with vodka and the raspberries with blackberries or damsons.

Use a muslin bag to strain the alcohol and fruits. Suspend the muslin with two bamboo sticks and collect the alcohol in a bowl.

# Chicken doorstop

★ ★ ★    LEVEL OF DIFFICULTY

This recycled doorstop makes a delightfully useful gift and brightens up any doorway. Look for textured upholstery samples or old, unwanted tweed clothes to use as fabric for the chicken's body, or go for something completely different and use brightly colored and patterned fabrics. If you don't have a sewing machine, sew the tail and wing feather shapes on in wool using chain stitch.

## materials

- Templates *(pp.340-41)*
- Recycled textured fabric, or samples
- Brown felt
- Red felt
- Scissors
- Sewing machine
- Stiff, recycled cardboard, cut to the same size as the base shape of the doorstop
- Sealed recycled plastic bag filled with about 2 lb 4 oz (1 kg) sand, rice grains, or barley grains
- Recycled sacking, rags, or an old towel for the filling
- Cotton thread and needle
- 2 recycled buttons

**1** Cut two body shapes from the textured fabric, two head shapes and one base shape from brown felt, and one wattle and comb from red felt.

**2** Sew on tail and wing details in zig-zag stitch. Align and sew the body shapes, correct sides facing inwards, up to the neck. Sew on the base shape.

**3** Turn the body inside out, insert the cardboard, position it over the base, place bag of sand over the card, and pack body with sacking.

**4** Sew the two head shapes, comb and wattle together, correct sides facing out. Stuff the head, sew it onto the neck, and sew buttons on for eyes.

# Make a vintage fabric box

★ ★ ★   LEVEL OF DIFFICULTY

It's sometimes hard to find attractive storage boxes among the mass of plastic home office equipment on sale, but a recycled box covered in vintage fabric will turn an everyday object into a stylish item for someone to use and display on their shelves. A large recycled boot or shoe box is ideal; try asking for any unwanted boxes in a shoe shop if you don't have any at home.

**1** Wrap the fabric, correct side facing out, around the box base and sides (p.187). Fold the top edges of the fabric and glue them neatly to the inside rim.

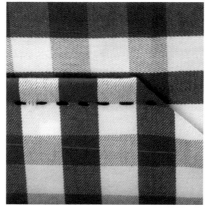

**2** Fold over the point of each triangular-shaped flap at either end and stitch the flap onto the box using running stitch.

**3** Cover the lid in the same way, but sew across the top of the lid. Glue the paper over one half of the lid. Glue the edges to the inside rim.

**4** Glue the ribbon around the edge of the lid and secure it in a bow. You can also cover boxes with themed pictures from vintage magazines.

## materials

- Empty recycled shoe or boot cardboard box and fitted lid
- 2 pieces of recycled vintage fabric, one piece cut just a little larger than the base and sides of the box, and the other cut just a little larger than the top and sides of the lid
- Embroidery thread and needle
- Eco-friendly adhesive glue
- Illustrated pages torn from an old, unwanted magazine (optional)
- Recycled ribbon

# Relaxing bath oil

★ ★ ★   LEVEL OF DIFFICULTY

This simple organic bath oil recipe can be easily adapted to make a luxuriously soothing bath oil or an invigorating bath oil, just by changing the essential oils you use. Package the bottled oils in a recycled box lined with colored tissue papers and include some of the ingredients for a rustic finish, or simply tie a length of beautiful vintage ribbon around the neck of each bottle.

## materials

- 2fl oz (50 ml) sweet almond oil
- 1 pretty recycled bottle and lid, sterilized *(p.125)*
- 10 drops of sandalwood essential oil
- 5 drops of jasmine essential oil
- 5 drops of orange essential oil
- 1 label

**For Soothing bath oil**

- 10 drops of rose essential oil
- 5 drops of chamomile essential oil
- 5 drops of lavender essential oil

**For Invigorating bath oil**

- 10 drops of grapefruit essential oil
- 5 drops of lemon essential oil
- 5 drops of juniper essential oil

**1** Carefully decant the almond oil from a measuring cup into the sterilized bottle.

**2** Add each of the different essential oils, drop by drop, to the almond oil in the bottle.

**3** Screw on the lid firmly and shake the bottle until the ingredients are well blended.

**4** Attach a label identifying the oil, and with instructions to add 1 tablespoon of the oil to a warm bath.

# Forage for chestnuts

If you want to add a bag of chestnuts to a Christmas gift basket, or if you love roasting fresh chestnuts over an open fire or including their unique flavor in your cooking, why not forage for them in fall? The sweet taste and floury consistency of chestnuts is transformed by being roasted, and they are so versatile that they taste good in both sweet and savory dishes.

Sweet chestnut trees *(Castanea sativa)* are commonly found in woodlands, parks, and deciduous forests. Once you know what to search for, they are relatively easy to find: look out for medium to large deciduous trees with glossy, dark green serrated leaves that turn yellow and drop off in fall as their prickly husks, each containing three edible nuts, fall to the ground. The bark on the trees often has deep furrows or fissures that spiral up the tree trunk, and they can grow up to 100 feet (30 m) in height and two 6 feel (2 m) in diameter. They also need a mild climate and adequate moisture for a good nut harvest, and dislike excessively wet and cold habitats. Sweet chestnut trees shouldn't be confused with horse-chestnut trees *(Aesculus)*, which produce inedible conkers in spiky cases.

## Gathering the nuts

The nuts begin falling in September, but these first fruits often aren't yet fully ripe. The ripest nuts usually fall between October and November, and should be plumper and a deep reddish brown color all over, except for the tip. As soon as the husks hit the ground, start collecting them to prevent the nuts deteriorating. Step gently on the husks to open them, and wear gardening gloves to extract the nuts. Discard any that are damaged or cracked. Store the nuts for up to a month in a cool, dry larder, or hang them up in an onion bag to keep the air circulating around them. Always cook the nuts before eating them, as they shouldn't be eaten raw.

## Cooking chestnuts

- **Use a sharp knife** to make a small incision at the tip of each nut, or they will explode as they heat up. Cut through the shell and just into the flesh.

- **Roast the nuts** in the oven or on an open fire. To cook them in an oven, roast them for about half an hour at 350°F (180°C) or until you can smell their sweet aroma.

- **If you want to roast** the nuts over a fire, you'll need a cast-iron pan. Place the prepared nuts in the pan and shake them occasionally over a medium flame for about 15 minutes.

- **Allow the nuts to cool** for a short while until you can handle them easily without burning your fingers. Remove the shells and the papery, rather bitter, inner skins before eating or using in a recipe.

- **If you can't forage** for fresh chestnuts, buy them fresh from grocers throughout the Christmas season, or purchase them dried, canned, or vacuum-packed from good shops or online and use them in your recipes.

# Cotton bag

★ ★ ★  LEVEL OF DIFFICULTY

This bucket bag is incredibly useful—it makes an ideal day bag, and is perfect for taking to the beach. By using two attractive, contrasting fabrics, you can reverse the bag accordingly; this double thickness also makes the bag much stronger. The pretty patchwork fabric creates an extra level of work, but if you want to simplify things slightly, use a single piece of fabric instead.

## materials

- Templates *(pp.342–43)*
- Scraps of cotton fabric, cut into squares and rectangles of various sizes and sewn into a large piece of patchwork *(p.150)*, with all the seams pressed flat using an iron
- An old gingham tablecloth, or similar material, for the lining
- Scissors
- Pins
- Sewing machine (optional)
- Cotton thread and needle

**1** Make up the templates according to the size you want the bag to be, and cut out two bag shapes from each piece of fabric so that you have four bag shapes altogether. Then cut two base shapes from each piece of fabric.

**2** Lay one patchwork shape on top of a gingham shape, correct sides facing inward. Stitch the curved edges only together on each side. Repeat with the other two shapes.

**3** Align the half-sewn shapes, with the patchwork on the outside. Lift the gingham. Sew the patchwork straight sides. Sew on the patchwork base, correct side facing inward.

**4** Lift the patchwork. Sew one straight side of gingham fabric. Partly sew the other side, leaving a gap of 6 in (15 cm). Sew on gingham base, correct side facing inward.

**5** Push all the fabrics through the gap in the gingham material to turn them the right way around. The seams should now all be hidden.

**6** Hand-sew the gap in the gingham fabric. The fabric shapes should now all be joined together, apart from the handle. Sew the patchwork handle ends together.

**7** Turn the handle over. Neatly sew the gingham handle ends together so that no seams show. You should now have one large handle and a complete, reversible bag.

# Mulled-wine kit

★ ★ ★    LEVEL OF DIFFICULTY

Red wine that has been heated, or mulled, and flavored is a well-loved Christmas drink, and a mulled-wine kit is the perfect present for someone who enjoys its warming, spicy undertones. When you tie the spice sachet to the bottle, add a gift label with instructions for making the mulled wine and what other ingredients to add. One kit should be enough for about six glasses.

**1** Prepare the spices: break the cinnamon stick into three pieces, crush the cardamom pods lightly, and grate a little fresh nutmeg.

**2** Place the cinnamon, cardamom, nutmeg, and cloves in the center of the cheesecloth square. Measure out the ginger and add it to the spices.

**3** Gather the four corners of the cheesecloth and hold them with the fingertips of one hand. Gather up the four remaining corners.

**4** Wrap the piece of twine around the top of the sachet and secure it tightly. Then tie the loose ends of the twine around the neck of the bottle.

## materials

- 1 cinnamon stick
- 6 cardamom pods, lightly crushed
- Fresh nutmeg
- 12 cloves
- 1 square cheesecloth, about 7 x 7 in (18 x 18 cm)
- 1 pinch ground ginger
- A length of twine
- 1 bottle red wine

**Mulled wine instructions**
Put the wine, sachet, half a cup (150 ml) of water, and 6 tablespoons granulated or demerara sugar into a pan. Heat gently until the sugar has dissolved, but don't allow the wine to come to the boil. Good ingredients to add: a splash of brandy, gin, Cointreau, or port, the juice of 1 orange, and 1 orange and 1 lemon, each sliced and cut into segments.

# Potted bulbs

★ ★ ★   LEVEL OF DIFFICULTY

Prepare ahead if you want to pot up bulbs as gifts that will flower in time for Christmas: August and September are the latest times to plant hyacinth, narcissi, and amaryllis bulbs for December flowering. If you time it just right, some of the bulbs will be beginning to open and just starting to release their fragrant perfume as you give them away.

## materials

- Selection of bulbs
- Some broken rocks or pebbles
- Organic, peat-free, multi-purpose compost
- Coconut matting pots, or other containers
- Pot labels
- Water

### 🌿 Green tip

**Use peat-free compost**
Peatlands are a precious habitat to plants, animals, and insects. Gardening is one of the greatest threats to peatlands, as most composts are peat-based. Buy "peat-free" or "peat-reduced" compost, or make your own compost.

**1** Select the containers and bulbs you would like to use: hyacinths, 'Paper White' narcissi, cyclamen, and amaryllis are all good choices.

**2** Lay some crocks in the base of a pot and fill halfway with compost. Shake the pot slightly to settle the soil. Place a bulb, or bulbs, in the pot.

**3** Fill with compost. Plant narcissi at twice their depth, cyclamen and hyacinths with their tips visible, and half-cover an amaryllis bulb.

**4** Firm the earth around the bulbs. Water and label each pot. Keep the potted bulbs cool, and hyacinths in a dark room, until the leaves show.

# Sew a pair of felt slippers

★ ★ ★   LEVEL OF DIFFICULTY

These cosy homemade slippers make an ideal gift for a child, but find out his or her shoe size first so that the slippers will fit properly. The templates illustrated on pages 335–37 are based on a child's 11½ shoe size (European size 30), so enlarge or reduce the template accordingly. Use soft material, such as a shrunken woollen scarf, so that the slippers feel really comfortable.

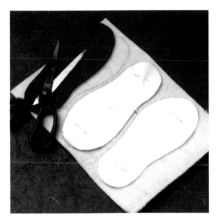

**1** Cut out two left feet and two right feet from the thick white felt. Then cut out one left foot and one right foot from the red felt.

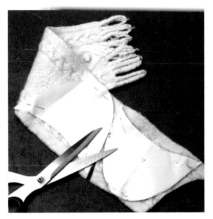

**2** Cut one left and one right upper from the scarf using the other template. You should now have three cut-outs for each foot, and two uppers.

**3** Pin the right upper to one of the white right soles and sew the two pieces together at the edge with white wool using running stitch.

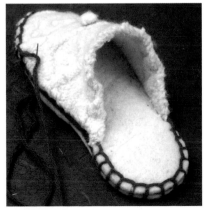

**4** Align the three felt soles, pin them together, then sew together using colored wool and blanket stitch. Repeat with the left slipper.

## materials

- Templates *(pp.335–37)*
- Thick felt for the soles, in two different colors
- Shrunken woollen scarf or pieces of colored felt for the uppers
- Pins
- Scissors
- White wool, colored wool, and a large darning needle

### 🍃 Green tip

**Buy your gifts locally**
If you don't have time to make many of your own gifts, buy them locally—reducing the amount imported from overseas. If you shop in your local community, you'll support small suppliers and minimize your carbon footprint.

## Mixed Christmas basket

To make up a spectacular gift basket *(p.190)* of sweet and savory homemade produce, include a bottle each of flavored alcohol and flavored oil *(pp.124–25)*, chocolate brownies *(pp.126–27)*, cookies *(pp.236–37)*, marshmallows *(pp.260–61)*, a jar each of chutney and jam *(pp.132–35)*, and a bag of sweet chestnuts.

# Wrap gifts creatively

It may be tempting to buy rolls of cheap, shiny paper to wrap your gifts, but this easy option won't reflect the care you've put into choosing the gifts themselves, and it doesn't benefit the planet: wrapping paper constitutes one of the biggest sources of waste over Christmas. So use thoughtfully chosen recycled materials to create elegant or amusingly wrapped presents.

## Waste paper facts

• **The UK alone produces** an extra three million tons of waste over the Christmas period, most of which is wrapping paper, packaging, and cards, which could all be recycled.

• **It has been calculated** that approximately 50,000 trees are felled each year to make the 8,000 tons of wrapping paper the UK uses—the equivalent of 32 sq miles (83 sq km). If just half of the wrapping paper currently thrown away was recycled, 25,000 trees would be saved.

• **The UK is currently** one of the least wooded countries in Europe: just 12 percent of the UK is now covered in wooded areas, compared to an average of 44 percent in other European countries.

## Reuse paper and cardboard

Gifts wrapped in reused paper can look stylish and unique if you wrap them with care: collect brown paper, out-of-date maps and atlases, or old wall charts, calendars, and unused rolls of wallpaper to build up a collection of instant Christmas wrapping. Pages from newspapers or magazines also make attractively wrapped gifts: use the sports section of a newspaper to wrap a gift for a sports fan, for example, or colorful comics to wrap gifts for children and teenagers. If your gift is an unusual shape, put it in a decorated or covered shoe box or shirt box, or use recycled paper sandwich bags decorated with dried leaves, pressed home-grown flowers, or feathers.

## Paper-free wrapping

A fun, quirky way to wrap a few of your favorite bulbs for an aspiring gardener is to place them inside one terracotta pot, place an identical upturned pot on top of it, and decorate the joined rims with a length of trailing ivy. It's the ultimate in eco-friendly wrapping, as the bulbs can be planted in the pots, and then the pots recycled indefinitely. You could also use vintage fabric or old, unwanted garments to wrap gifts: a length of velvet, an old scarf, cloth napkin, handkerchief, or tea towel can all be transformed into stylish gift wrap. Tie the gift with another recycled garment, such as a thin scarf or tie. Or make your own giftbags with scraps of fabric *(p.150)*—a simple drawstring bag made out of pretty fabric can become a gift in itself.

# Recycled gift wrapping

★ ★ ★   **LEVEL OF DIFFICULTY**

Part of the pleasure of being given an imaginatively wrapped, beautifully presented gift is guessing just what might be underneath all the wrapping. If your gift is an unusual shape, put it in a discarded box first and then take the trouble to wrap the gift carefully, so that the recycled materials you choose will look their best.

**1** Put the gift in the box; shapes with flat, angular sides are easier to wrap neatly. Place the box in the center of the paper.

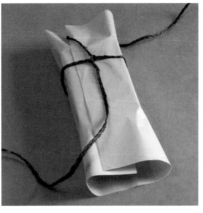

**2** Fold two sides of the paper over the box so they overlap. Wrap the string around the box and tie it in a knot to hold the folded paper in place.

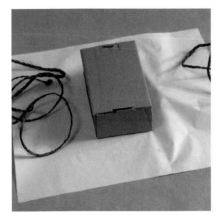

**3** Fold the paper carefully at each end of the box: press the paper neatly in toward the center to create two triangular flaps at either end.

**4** Fold down the flaps so they overlap. Wrap the string over the flaps to hold them in place, turn the box over, and secure the string in a bow.

## materials

- Recycled cardboard box large enough to hold the gift (optional)
- Clean sheet of recycled paper, ironed on a low setting to get rid of creases
- Colored string or ribbon (iron the ribbon on a low setting, or run through heated hair straighteners, to get rid of any creases)

### 🍃 Green tip

**Avoid sticky tape**
Paper can't be reused if it is covered in sticky tape, so use ribbon, upholstery trimmings, twine, raffia, wool, or string instead. Use paper-based, water-activated gummed tape to post a gift; duct tape has a negative environmental impact.

# Gift wrapping variations

**Tea towel and vintage tartan ribbon** Use a colorful tea towel and smart ribbon—the tea towel could even form part of the gift.

**Paper and corrugated cardboard** Over-wrap recycled paper with ridged cardboard for textural interest. Secure with a ribbon.

**Newspaper and garden string** Sheets of newspaper are a simple option, but look stylish. Tie with green string for a festive look.

**Tissue paper and leaves** Arrange leaves between sheets of recycled tissue paper. Secure the wrapping with glue and string.

**Printed paper** Tear pages from an old atlas, a map of a well-loved area, or a color magazine to make this unusual wrapping.

**Brown paper and woven string** Use recycled brown paper and make an attractive ribbon by weaving together lengths of string.

**Vintage fabric and string** Use trimmed oddments of beautiful fabric to wrap gifts. Tie simply with festively colored string.

**Recycled shirt** Cut the back off an old shirt and wrap the shirt front around the gift. Secure the sleeves on top with string.

# Decorate gifts

Sometimes the smallest touches make all the difference, and a pile of packages under the tree can look so much more enticing if they are thoughtfully decorated. Be creative by choosing natural and recycled everyday items and trimmings instead of the usual ready-made, bought alternatives to make your wrapped gifts look special.

## Create a gift basket

- **A recycled basket**, or one made of willow or wicker from sustainable sources, makes an ideal basket.

- **Line the hamper** with plenty of natural material like hay or straw.

- **Decorate jars and bottles** of home-made produce with vintage fabric and ribbon. Fill small linen sacks with nuts, fresh herbs, or cookies.

- **Arrange the produce** on the hay so that all the labels are clearly visible.

- **Cut a few lengths** of holly or mistletoe and tuck them inside the rim of the basket around the gifts.

## Recycled and vintage items

Save brightly colored ribbon from your own gifts and purchases, or look out for vintage ribbon, iron it with a cool iron or pull it through a pair of heated hair straighteners, and tie it around gifts wrapped in brown paper. If you have a few old beads and buttons, sew or glue them onto the ribbon to create a charming, detailed effect, or thread them onto string or twine and secure the ends in a knot.

## Natural raffia

Raffia is made from mulberry tree bark, which regenerates, so no trees are cut down to produce it. Gather a few lengths of raffia together, or plait them, wrap them around a gift, and tie them in an extravagant bow.

## Found materials

Collect attractive natural materials and fresh foliage: pine cones, holly leaves, trailing ivy, sprigs of bright berries, dried leaves (p.16), sliced dried fruit (p.65), and cinnamon sticks all make lovely and unique final touches when tied on top of gifts.

## Gift tags

Cut festive motifs from recycled patterned paper, felt, or fabric and stick or sew them onto luggage labels or small pieces of card to make gift tags; they will look much more striking than bought labels. Alternatively, stick on dried star anise and cardamom pods in simple patterns for delightfully aromatic gift tags.

# Decorated gift variations

**Cinnamon sticks and plaited raffia** Tie the gift with plaited raffia, thread ribbon under the raffia, and tie it around cinnamon sticks.

**Evergreen foliage and string** Gather a few lengths of string, tie up the gift, and tuck a couple of sprigs of foliage under the bow.

**Pine cones and raffia** Tie the gift with raffia, wrap a little thin wire around the base of each cone, and tie them to the bow.

**Dried fruits and raffia** Glue three dried orange slices together in an overlapped row, tie the gift with raffia, and glue on the slices.

**Raffia and dried leaves** Gather a few lengths of raffia, tie the gift, and glue on a few dried, flattened leaves just under the bow.

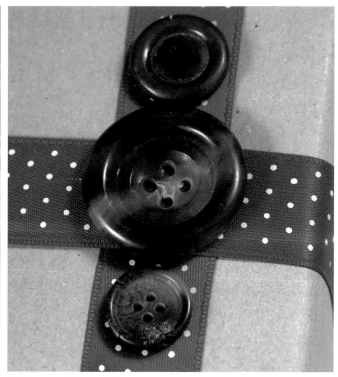

**Ribbons and buttons** Wrap recycled ribbon around the gift and glue different-sized buttons onto the ribbon.

**Holly sprig and vintage ribbon** Tie the gift with bright vintage ribbon and tuck a holly sprig with a few berries under the bow.

**Threaded buttons** Thread odd buttons onto a very thin length of ribbon and tie the ribbon around the gift.

# Gift label variations

**Dried leaf star label** Glue a dried, flattened leaf *(p. 16)* onto recycled cardboard, cut a star shape, glue a nut in the center..

**Fabric star label** Glue some cheery fabric onto recycled card, cut into a star shape, and glue on a dried bay leaf and old button.

**Mini star gift tag** Cut out a fabric star, glue it onto folded cardboard, decorate with a button and a little raffia loop.

**Rustic bead label** Push both ends of a length of garden string through a hole, thread beads onto each end, and tie in a knot.

**Skeleton leaf label** Thread a piece of string through the hole of a label and glue a couple of dried, flattened leaves over the hole.

**Paper dove label** Cut a dove template from recycled cardboard, glue on festive-looking recycled paper, and cut it out.

**Paper holly leaf label** Cut a holly leaf shape (p.325) out of recycled paper, glue onto recycled cardboard, add a berry button.

**Fresh holly leaf label** Sew a holly leaf onto a luggage label with festive-colored embroidery thread using simple running stitch.

TABLE

# Natural candleholders

★ ★ ★  LEVEL OF DIFFICULTY

A table illuminated by candlelight creates a wonderfully intimate and relaxed atmosphere. For some striking and unusual candle holders, use dried artichoke or cardoon (artichoke thistle) heads. Pick the dried flower heads in fall before the weather turns, then leave them to air-dry a little longer in a cool, dry place. Never leave these candles unattended when lit.

## materials

- Dried globe artichoke (*Cynara cardunculus Scolymus*) or cardoon (*Cynara cardunculus*) heads
- Garden shears
- Thin wire
- Scissors
- 1 candle
- Empty tealight container or recycled tin foil
- Eco-friendly adhesive glue

**1** Cut down the stem of the artichoke or cardoon with a pair of shears so that it sits level when placed on a flat surface.

**2** Wind one end of the wire around the stem. Wrap the wire twice around the head to hold the leaves in place and secure it again at the base.

**3** Cut out the choke in the center of the flower head with a pair of scissors to make a hole just large enough for a candle to fit into.

**4** Cover the base of the candle with the empty tealight container or foil. Glue the candle into the hole. Make more holders in the same way.

### Green tip

**Choose natural candles**
Many candles are made from paraffin, which is derived from petroleum (a non-renewable source), and are not biodegradable. Choose eco-friendly natural soy and beeswax candles, which are made from renewable sources and are clean-burning.

TABLE **199**

# Glass jar candleholders

★ ★ ★    LEVEL OF DIFFICULTY

Candles are essential at Christmas time as they bring an extra sense of warmth, so dot these pretty tealight candleholders around a table or along a windowsill and light the candles as dusk falls. Decorate the jars with leaves and seed heads, or other simple decorations, and tie on ribbons that echo the colors in your room. Don't leave these candles unattended.

## materials

- Several recycled jam jars, baby-food jars, or similiar
- Strong wire
- Selection of leaves and seed heads, either fresh or dried *(p.16)*
- Eco-friendly adhesive glue
- Recycled ribbon
- Several tealights

🍂 **Green tip**

**Recycle old candles**
Heat waste candles in a pan over a gentle heat. Lift out the dead wicks and cut a new wick just longer than your mold (try using an old teacup or glass). Soak in the wax. Pour the wax into the lightly oiled mold, ensuring the wick is at the center. Leave to set.

**1** Clean the jars thoroughly and dry them. Put the lids aside. Cut a length of wire just larger than the diameter of the neck of a jar.

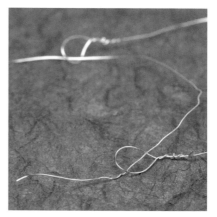

**2** Cut a second length of wire about 12 in (30 cm) long. Make a secure loop at either end. Thread the first length of wire through each loop.

**3** Wrap the short length of wire around the neck of the jar and secure it tightly. Adjust the loops so that the wire handle works correctly.

**4** Glue leaves or seed heads onto the sides of the jar. Tie a ribbon around the neck and slip a tealight into the jar. Then decorate other jars.

# Vintage fabric placemats

★ ★ ★   LEVEL OF DIFFICULTY

Create a really festive look at your table with these fabric placemats: they are designed to be reversible so that they are longer-lasting. You could use one side of the mat for meals through the year and save the other side for special occasions and celebration meals. Choose simple, traditional fabric for a rustic look, or source elegantly patterned linen for a more sophisticated feel.

**1** Cut four oblong pieces, each 13 x 9 in (33 x 23 cm), from the interfacing, four from the hand towels, and four from the tablecloth.

**2** Align a piece of gingham and linen, correct sides facing each other. Place a piece of interfacing on the back of the linen. Pin together.

**3** Sew the three fabrics together with a seam of ½ in (1 cm) round the edges,. Leave a gap along one side to turn the fabric the right way round.

**4** Turn the placemat inside out so the interfacing is hidden inside. Sew up the gap in the fabric. Repeat the process with the other placemats.

## materials

**To make four placemats**

- Interfacing
- 4 old-fashioned linen hand towels or tea towels
- An old tablecloth in gingham (optional)
- Scissors
- Pins
- Cotton thread and needle or sewing machine

### 🌿 Craft tip

**Matching name cards**
Cut ½ x 2½ in (1 x 6 cm) strips of vintage fabric with pinking shears. Tie the strips in bows or simple knots. Tear a 4 x 3 in (10 x 8 cm) square of recycled cardboard, score and fold it *(p.120)*, glue bow in the corner, write on name, and place by a setting.

# Edible place-name cards

★★★  LEVEL OF DIFFICULTY

These dark, richly spiced Scandinavian ginger cookies may take a little longer to prepare than other cookie recipes, but the wait is well worth it. They not only make fun place-name cards with your guests' initials or names written on in white icing, they are also a delicious combination of spicy, crunchy sweetness. Make any extra dough into smaller cookie shapes to be eaten another time.

## ingredients

**Makes about 16 cookies**

Preheat the oven to 400°F (200°C)

Bake for 5–8 minutes

- 7 oz (200 g) butter
- ¾ cup sugar syrup
- ¾ cup sugar
- 1–2 tsp ground cinnamon
- 1–2 tsp ground cloves
- 1–2 tsp ground ginger
- Grated zest of 1 orange
- 2 eggs
- 1 lb 2 oz (510 g) flour
- 3 tsp baking powder

**For the icing**

Use confectioner's sugar mixed with a little warm water to make a paste. Spoon the icing into a small recycled plastic bag with one small corner cut off, squeeze the icing out gently, and write names or initials on the cooled cookies.

**1** Put the butter, syrup, sugar, spices, and orange zest into a saucepan. Bring the mixture to the boil briefly and then allow to cool.

**2** Beat the eggs into the cooled mixture, one at a time, and mix thoroughly. Then sift the flour and baking powder into a large bowl.

**3** Add the wet mix to the flour, a little at a time, combine into a dough, wrap tightly in eco-friendly plastic wrap, and refrigerate overnight.

**4** Take off the plastic wrap, roll out the dough to ⅛ in (3 mm) depth, cut into shapes, place on a greased baking tray, and bake in the oven.

# Pear place-name holders

★ ★ ★    LEVEL OF DIFFICULTY

These unusual cardamom pear place-name holders give a lovely spicy-sweet scent, and look stunning arranged along the center of a set table. Choose ripe, but not overripe, pears so that their skins are just soft enough for the pods to be pushed through. You can, if you prefer, omit the twigs and rest small cards with handwritten menus in between the pods at the top of each pear.

**1** Select a pear and press the pointed end of a cardamom pod gently into the flesh. Press more pods in as closely to each other as possible.

**2** Continue to gently press the pods into the pear flesh until the skin is covered completely in pods.

**3** Once covered, the pear should be able to stand upright unaided. Leave a small gap in the top of the pear and insert the twig.

**4** Tear a small rectangle of paper and write a guest's initials on it. Rest the paper between the "V" shape of the twig. Then make up more pears.

## materials

**For each place-name holder**

- 1 ripe pear
- A quantity of green cardamom pods
- 1 twig with two stems forming a "V" shape at one end
- Recycled paper

### 🍃 Green tip

**Avoid packaging**
Much food produce is now heavily packaged, which is costly and usually unnecessary. Try to buy your pears loose and choose a simply packaged bag of cardamom pods to avoid any wasteful plastic packaging.

TABLE **209**

# Evergreen centerpiece

★ ★ ★  LEVEL OF DIFFICULTY

A special seasonal foliage centerpiece will dress your table perfectly and set the scene for a festive meal. Evergreen foliage such as bay and conifer will last well and look fresher for longer than some other seasonal varieties, but choose whatever you have available in the yard, or can buy, to make the best-looking table display.

## materials

- Deep, fluted baking dish or bundt tin
- 1 large candle
- Small bunches of evergreen foliage, such as bay and conifer
- Shears
- Thin garden wire
- A few pine cones

**1** Place the baking dish on a flat, level surface. Use a dish with a fixed, rather than a removable, base, so that water won't leak out of it.

**2** Position the candle in the center of the dish. If you wish, you can stick the candle into place, but use a waterproof glue to do this.

**3** Cut the conifer foliage into small bundles using shears. Tie wire around each bundle and place them in the dish around the candle.

**4** Insert other foliage in between the conifer bundles. Position the pine cones around the candles and add a little water to keep the foliage fresh.

## Herb variation

Gather a selection of fresh, seasonal herbs such as rosemary, sage, thyme, and bay leaves, and use them to create an alternative table centrepiece *(pp.210–211)*.

# Decorated chair backs

These simple arrangements, made up of a few stems of trailing ivy *(Hedera)*, mistletoe *(Viscum album)*, and holly *(Ilex)*, roughly tied together with natural raffia, and attached to the back of each chair, will lend a lovely rustic detail to your decorated table.

# Use organic table linen

Beautiful table linen is the most inviting way to dress your table, no matter what the occasion. Whether you choose a vibrant tablecloth or a pure linen cloth and napkins, they all create the same pleasing effect. Conventional cotton production uses toxic chemicals, so buy organic or vintage cotton linen and enjoy the reassuringly natural quality that we typically associate with this material.

Industrially grown cotton is responsible for over a quarter of the world's pesticide and fertilizer use, but organic cotton production offers a solution to this problem by using natural pesticides—which often contain a mixture of chilli, garlic, and soap—and intercropping, where a natural barrier of secondary crops is grown in and around small plots of cotton crops. Both of these methods deter pests from ruining the cotton crops without destroying the pests' natural predators. Organic cotton production is also less water-intensive than conventional cotton production and so promotes better water management.

## Choosing organic table linens

Organic cotton may cost slightly more than conventionally grown cotton, but it means that farmers get a fairer price for their produce. Look for a Fairtrade mark, which guarantees this fair and stable price for farmers and farm workers in developing countries. The increase in consumer demand for organic cotton means that its output and availability is expanding rapidly; source organic linen from reliable internet websites if you can't yet buy it locally. An equally low-impact alternative is to buy vintage, which is often one-of-a-kind and has a comfortingly nostalgic, faded quality that makes your table look unique. Dry undyed organic linen in the sun to bleach it naturally, but keep colored and patterned fabrics away from direct sunlight, and store the linen in clean cupboards with a few natural moth-repellent sachets *(p.154)*.

## Cotton industry facts

- **Toxic chemicals** in pesticide sprays have a massive impact on farmers, the soil, and surrounding wildlife through water contamination or exposure to the spray. According to the World Health Organisation, pesticides unintentionally inhaled or absorbed through the skin by cotton workers in developing countries result in 20,000 deaths, and three million people with health problems, every year.

- **In India**, cotton production accounts for only five percent of the land, but 54 percent of its annual pesticide use.

- **Eight times** more pesticide is sprayed on 2.5 acres (1 hectare) of land planted with a cotton crop than on a similar plot planted with a conventional food crop.

- **Once the world's** fourth-largest inland lake, the Aral Sea in central Asia has shrunk to 15 percent of its original size, mainly as a result of cotton crop irrigation. Between 1960 and 2000, the amount of water diverted from rivers feeding the Aral Sea doubled as cotton production in the area increased. The negative impact on the Aral Sea's once-thriving fishing industry has been dramatic.

TABLE **219**

# Dried napkin decoration

Make a simple napkin decoration by gluing together a dried leaf, a dried orange slice, and a cinnamon stick. Rest it lightly on a folded linen napkin, or secure it with a length of natural raffia.

## Fresh napkin decoration

Gather a few short stems of fresh mistletoe and a sprig of two of bright berries, bind them together with some garden twine, and rest the small posy on a folded linen napkin.

# Play traditional games

These games will provide hours of entertainment around the dining table after a meal is over. They are all easy to play, require little space, no special equipment, and can be easily adapted to suit almost any age group, which makes them fun for everyone to play.

## Guess Who?

This game is suitable for four or more players. The only equipment you need is small pieces of paper and pencils. Most age groups can play.

**The rules:**
The game can be played in two ways.
1. Each player writes their name on a piece of paper, folds it, and places it in a container. One player takes a folded piece of paper from the container, silently reads the name, and assumes the character and mannerisms of the person whose name is on the paper. The others must try to identify who is being imitated.

2. All the players discreetly write down on separate pieces of paper the names of as many famous people—dead or alive, real or fictional—as they can think of. All paper should be folded and put in a container. The players divide into teams and each team take turns to play for 30 seconds at a time. One player is the "caller," picking a piece of paper out of the container and using any words or actions to describe the person, except mentioning their name. The team must guess the name as quickly as possible and move on to the next piece of paper. The team with the most correctly guessed names wins the game.

## I Went to Market

A simple memory game for two or more players. Impose a time limit if you wish.

**The rules:**
One player starts by saying, "I went to market and I bought...", and adds an item. The next player repeats the phrase, including the first item, and adds a second item. Each player takes it in turns to repeat the existing phrase and add another item. If any player omits an item, or places it in the incorrect order, they drop out of the round.

## Proverbs

Suitable for three or more players, but not for smaller children. No equipment is required, and the game can last as long as you wish.

**The rules:**
One player leaves the room while the others agree on a well-known proverb, such as "A little knowledge is a dangerous thing." The player is invited back into the room and can ask the other players any questions they like. The first player questioned must include the first word of the proverb in their answer, the second player must use the second, and so on. The questioner has to guess the proverb as quickly as possible (a time limit can be set for each player if you wish).

# In the Manner of the Word

Suitable for four or more adults and older, but not smaller, children. No equipment is required, and the game can last as long as you wish.

## The rules:

One player leaves the room and those remaining choose an adverb: for example, sadly, mischievously, heavily. The player returns to the room and has to guess what the adverb is, either by asking questions that the others have to answer "in the manner of the word," or by asking any of them to act out a situation, such as cooking.

Alternatively, two players can leave the room to think of an adverb. When they return, the others have to guess the adverb by giving the pair situations to act out. Many people prefer this version because it is less inhibiting.

# The Dictionary Game

Each team make up false definitions of obscure words and the opposing team has to separate the true meaning from the false. At least four people are needed to play, but it works best with six players. You'll need a good dictionary, pencils and paper. Allow about half an hour for each round.

## The rules:

Players form two teams. Each team picks an obscure word from the dictionary. One member writes down the real definition of the word while the others make up convincing false definitions. Each team reads out their definitions. The opposing team try to guess the true definition, and a point is awarded for each successful bluff.

# Twenty Questions

Also known as "Animal, vegetable, mineral," this classic guessing game is educational as well as fun, and encourages creative thinking, reasoning, and detective work. Ideally, you need a minimum of four players if you want to play in teams, but any number, and most age groups, can play. No equipment is required, and the game can last as long as you want it to.

## The rules:

These classifications should be explained to all the players before the game begins:

**Animal**: Includes animal products, such as milk, wool, leather etc., as well as individual people and animals.

**Vegetable**: Includes anything that is organic, but is not from an animal, for example, paper, wine, or flowers.

**Mineral**: Something that has never been alive, such as paint or a lamp.

One player thinks of an object and the opposing team are allowed 20 questions, including direct challenges, to find out what the word is. They must first ask whether it is animal, vegetable, or mineral.

If a player makes a challenge and guesses incorrectly, that player is out of the round. If all the players on the opposing team fail, the person who chose the word wins the round. Any player who guesses correctly can choose a new object and the next round begins. If an answer can be shown afterward to have been incorrect, that player is then disqualified from the game.

TABLE **223**

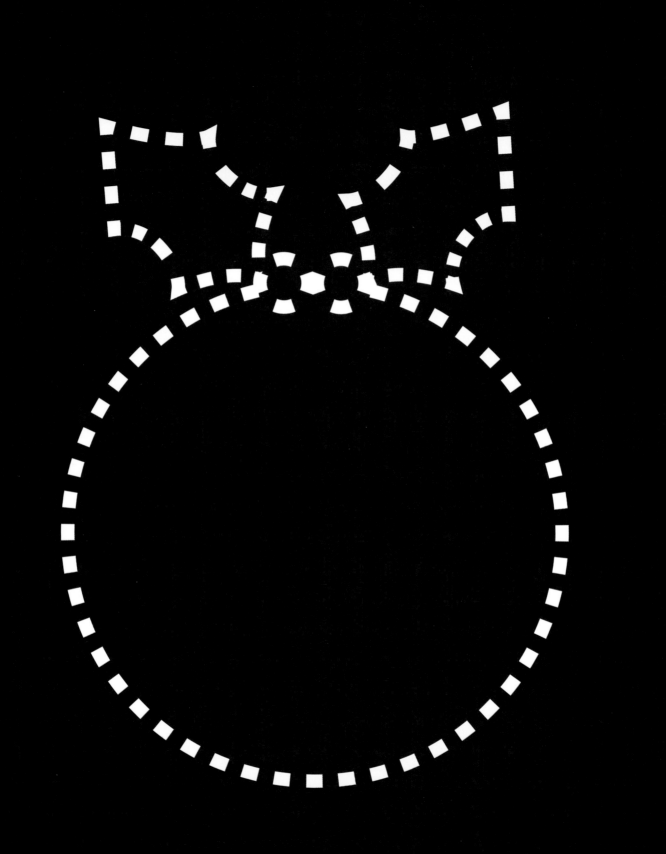

# FOOD

# Walnut bread

To help bread cook well, mist the inside of the oven with a water spray just before baking the dough. The loaf is cooked if it sounds hollow when tapped on the base. This walnut bread will keep in a bread safe for up to four days, and it also freezes well. If you want to reheat it in a low oven, rub a little water over it beforehand to prevent it from drying out as it warms up.

## ingredients

**Makes 2 ring loaves**

Preheat the oven to 450°F (230°C)

- 3¼ cups all-purpose white bread flour
- ¾ cup dark rye flour
- 1½ tsp dried yeast
- 2 tsp salt
- 1½ cups tepid water
- 2 cups walnuts, crushed

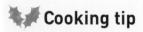 **Cooking tip**

**Kneading bread**
The action of kneading warms and stretches the gluten in flour. This elasticity, and the action of yeast, gives bread its light, springy texture. Press and stretch the dough away from you, then lift the edges into the middle, give it a quarter turn, and repeat.

**1** Mix the flours together, then add the yeast and salt. Add a little of the water (it should be tepid); mix the ingredients. Gradually add more water until the mixture becomes a dough.

**2** Add the nuts to the dough, knead the dough for 5–8 minutes until pliable, place it in a lightly oiled bowl, cover with a damp dishcloth, and leave it to rest until it doubles in size (p.230).

**3** Turn the rested dough out onto a clean, lightly floured surface again and divide it into two equal amounts. Knead each half of the dough into a tight ball.

**4** Shape each ball into a ring with a hole the size of a fist. Place on a lightly floured baking sheet and cover with a damp dishcloth until they double in size. Then bake for 20–25 minutes.

# Focaccia bread

This bread tastes so good that it's unlikely you'll have much left over after serving it, but it keeps well in a bread safe for two days or so. When you turn the bread out onto a wire rack to cool after baking, drizzle a little olive oil over the surface. The bread will soak up the oil as it cools to give even more flavor.

**1** Roast the bulbs, cut side down, for 20 minutes or until soft. Squeeze the cooked cloves from their skins into a small bowl. Mash lightly so that some cloves remain whole. Set aside.

**2** Put the flour in a bowl and make a well in the center. Add the yeast and salt, half the water, and all the oil. Using a fork, draw the flour from the edge of the bowl into the well.

**3** Stir in the rest of the water, bit by bit, until it forms a dough. Knead the dough for 5 minutes (p.226), then leave it in a clean, lightly floured, covered bowl to rest for 1 hour (p.230).

**4** Knock the air out of the dough. Spread it out in a floured baking tray, rub in the olive oil, scatter garlic and rosemary on top, and leave to rest, covered, for 30 minutes. Then bake.

## ingredients

Preheat the oven to 375°F (190°C) and bake for 20 minutes or until the surface is golden brown

- 3 whole bulbs garlic with their bases sliced off
- 1 lb 2 oz (500 g) white self-rising flour
- 1 tsp fast-action dried yeast
- 1 tsp salt
- 1¼ cups tepid water
- A good glug of olive oil— about ¼ cup
- Fresh rosemary leaves, chopped, from several rosemary sprigs

# Bread animals

This basic white bread recipe is ideal for children to make something edible, and shaping the dough into animals gives them the freedom to use their imagination. When the breads are ready to be baked, mist the inside of the oven with a water spray. They are cooked if they have an all-around golden tinge and sound hollow when tapped on the base.

## ingredients

Preheat the oven to 450°F (230°C)

- 1 lb 2 oz (500 g) all-purpose white bread flour
- 1 tsp dried yeast
- 1 tsp salt
- 1¼ cup tepid water
- Currants and pumpkin seeds for features and decoration

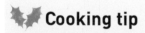

### Cooking tip

**Resting dough**
Covering dough with a damp dishcloth and leaving it to rest in a warm place for a period of time allows the yeast in the dough to do its work and make the bread light. With a little warmth and moisture, the active ingredients in the yeast release cardon dioxide gas, which raises the dough.

**1** Put the flour in a bowl, make a well in the center, and add the yeast and salt. Gradually add the water and stir with a fork to make a loose dough. Use your hands to form a ball.

**2** Turn the dough out onto a clean, lightly floured surface. Knead it for 8–10 minutes until it is elastic and pliable. Turn the dough gradually as you press and stretch it (p.226).

**3** Shape the dough into a ball and place in a lightly floured bowl. Cover with a damp dishcloth and leave to rest in a warm place for one hour. Then shape the dough into animals.

**4** Decorate the animals, put them on a lightly oiled baking tray, and cover with a damp tea towel. Leave to rest for 30 minutes. Bake for 15–20 minutes, then cool on a wire rack.

# Mince pies

Prepare the mincemeat ideally a week, or at the very least one day, ahead of making the pies to allow the flavors to develop. If the rolled pastry is too thick it won't cook quickly enough and the mincemeat will soak into it, turning it soggy; the right thickness results in a delicate, crispy pastry. These quantities should make 24 pies that will keep well for up to seven days in an airtight tin.

**1** Mix the mincemeat ingredients in a bowl, put in a sterilized jar *(p.132)*, and store in the fridge. For the pastry, mix the flour, butter and salt in a bowl. Add the egg and water. Form a dough.

**2** Turn the dough onto a lightly floured surface and knead until smooth. Chill for 10 minutes in the fridge, then roll it out to 1/16 in (2 mm) thick and cut 24 discs with a cutter.

**3** Preheat the oven to 375°F (190°C). Press each disc gently into the individual bases of a bun or pie tray. Fill each pastry case with a teaspoon of the mincemeat.

**4** Top the pies with pretty shapes cut from the remaining pastry dough. Brush each with a little milk, sprinkle with superfine sugar, and bake for 18–20 minutes or until golden.

## ingredients

**For the mincemeat**
- 3 oz (85 g) each golden raisins, raisins, and currants
- 1½ oz (35 g) blanched almonds, finely chopped
- ½ firm apple, cored and coarsely grated
- ½ cup raw sugar
- 2 oz (50 g) candied citron, chopped
- 2½ oz (75 g) dried cranberries
- Grated zest of 1 orange
- Grated zest of 1 lemon
- 1 tsp pumpkin pie spice
- 1½ oz (40 g) lard
- 2 fl oz (50 ml) brandy

**For the pastry**
- 2 cups all-purpose flour
- 1 stick butter, diced
- A large pinch of salt
- 1 large egg yolk
- 1–2 tbsp hot water
- 2 tbsp milk
- 1 tbsp superfine sugar

# Vanilla cookies

The melted candies in these cookies look like tiny stained-glass windows when they catch the light. Make a mixture of some plain cookies and some with sweet centers, and if you want to hang the cookies from your tree as edible decorations, make a small hole in the top of each shape before baking them. The sweet mix is very hot as the cookies come out of the oven, so take care.

## ingredients

**Makes 12 cookies**

Preheat the oven to 375°F (190°C)

- 1 stick butter
- 1¼ cups superfine sugar
- ½ tsp vanilla extract
- 2 eggs
- 4¾ cups all-purpose flour
- 2 tsp baking powder
- 2 tsp ground cinnamon
- ½ tsp salt
- A little milk
- A handful of organic hard candies, crushed (put candies of one color in a clean, recycled plastic bag and crush them with a rolling pin)

**1** Place buttered wax paper over two large baking sheets. Cream together the butter and sugar in a large bowl. Add the vanilla extract and stir in the eggs.

**2** Sift the flour, baking powder, cinnamon, and salt into a separate bowl. Add the egg mix and then the milk, a little at a time, and mix into a dough. Chill for 30 minutes.

**3** Roll out the dough on a lightly floured surface until ¼ in (5 mm) thick. Cut shapes using a cutter. Use a smaller cutter to make the holes, and fill each with a few crushed sweets.

**4** Bake for 10 minutes. Leave the baked cookies on the paper and transfer the paper onto a wire rack. Allow the cookies to cool completely before removing them from the paper.

# Prepare Christmas drinks

Winter is the time to enjoy warming drinks to keep the chilly weather at bay, so if you want to serve something other than Champagne or wine, try these fruity seasonal drinks. The Old-fashioned rum with a twist takes a little more time and care to prepare than the others, but it's worth the effort.

## Old-fashioned rum with a twist

Put the honey and 1 tablespoon of rum in a Rocks glass. Stir the mixture until the honey has mixed into the rum. Add 1 ice cube and 1 mint leaf and stir until the ice has nearly melted. Add another tablespoon of rum and another ice cube. Stir until the ice cube has partly melted. Add the rest of the rum and one more ice cube. Stir the drink 15 times or so and then fill the glass to the top with ice cubes. Take a piece of pared lime rind, crack it over the glass to release the oils from the skin, and serve.

## Spiced fruit cocktail

Peel and slice the pear and place it in the bottom of a cocktail shaker. Add the plum jam and ground cinnamon and muddle down (a muddler is a barman's wooden utensil used to crush hard ingredients to release flavors; the handle of a wooden spoon can be used instead). Add the Cognac, apple juice, and some ice. Shake and strain the mixture into a cocktail glass, add a few drops of lemon juice and serve.

## Fruit fizz

Put some ice cubes into a tall tumbler or highball glass. Pour in equal amounts of the orange and cranberry juice, and the lemonade. Stir well and serve.

### Drink recipes

- **Old-fashioned rum with a twist**
For each drink:

  - 2 tbsp sugar syrup
  - 2fl oz (50 ml) aged rum
  - Ice cubes
  - 1 fresh mint leaf
  - Pared lime rind, to garnish

- **Spiced fruit cocktail**
For each drink:

  - 1 pear
  - 1 tsp plum jam
  - 1 pinch ground cinnamon
  - 2fl oz (50 ml) Cognac
  - 2fl oz (50 ml) apple juice
  - Ice cubes
  - A few drops of fresh lemon juice

- **Fruit fizz**
For each drink:

  - Ice cubes
  - 1/3 glass fresh orange juice, chilled
  - 1/3 glass cranberry juice, chilled
  - 1/3 glass organic lemonade, chilled

# Christmas cake

Make this cake three months in advance, store it in several layers of baking parchment in an airtight tin, and gradually soak it with brandy over a series of weeks to ensure it has a great depth of flavor. If you don't like the taste of brandy, make the cake at least one week before you want to eat it. For a simple but effective icing sugar pattern on the cake, use a paper doily as a stencil.

## ingredients

Preheat the oven to 275°F (140°C)

- 1¼ cups currants
- 1 cup golden raisins
- 1 cup raisins
- ¾ cup (about 20) glacé cherries, rinsed, dried and quartered
- Packed ¼ cup (about 14) dried apricots, cut into pieces
- ¼ cup mixed candied citrus, finely chopped
- 4fl oz (100 ml) brandy
- 2 cups all-purpose flour
- 2 tsp grated nutmeg
- 2 tsp pumpkin pie spice
- 1 cup (2 sticks) butter, melted
- 1 cup dark muscovado sugar
- ½ cup whole almonds, chopped
- 1 tbsp molasses
- Zest and juice of 1 lemon
- Zest and juice of 1 orange
- 4 extra large eggs
- Brandy for soaking

**1** Place fruits in a bowl, add brandy, leave overnight. Grease and line a 8 in (20 cm) deep round cake pan, ensuring that the paper around the side is higher than the height of the pan.

**2** Measure the flour, spices, butter, sugar, almonds, molasses, and the lemon and orange zests and juice into a large bowl and add the brandy-soaked fruits.

**3** Add the eggs to the ingredients and mix everything together thoroughly. Then spoon the cake mixture into the prepared pan.

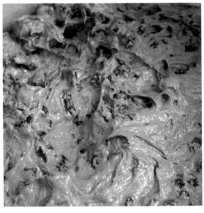

**4** Spread the mix out evenly with a palette knife and cover with a double layer of wax paper. Bake in the oven for about 4½ hours until firm. Allow to cool in the pan.

# Choose seasonal foods

Many of us are now so used to buying fruit and vegetables that have been air-freighted in from around the world that we are often unaware, or at best confused, about which foods are in season. As nice as it might seem to have our favorite fruit and vegetables available all year round, locally grown seasonal produce at its nutritional best is much tastier.

The convenience of modern supermarket shopping has meant that we now expect to be able to buy certain foods throughout the year, even when they are out of season. The flavor of such imported, out-of-season food is always inferior, and the impact of pollution and greenhouse gases created by transporting the produce from afar is damaging to the environment.

## Food at its best

The bonus of buying seasonal food from local producers is that the fruits or vegetables will have been allowed to ripen naturally. As a result, they'll contain more nutrients and generally have a better flavor than food that has been harvested early and ripened artificially. Most fruit and vegetables start to lose their flavor and nutritional value as soon as they've been picked, so buying local seasonal food guarantees you a shorter time from picking to eating. Out-of-season produce may have been picked six or more weeks before you buy it.

## Enjoy the variety

While some foods, such as bananas and mangoes, won't grow naturally in North America and Europe, and so can only be purchased as imported produce, there is a huge variety of fruits and vegetables that grow locally throughout the year. If you buy locally grown seasonal produce whenever you can, you'll end up with a more nutritious and tasty diet, while supporting local farmers.

## Storing home-grown winter vegetables

- **Keep root vegetables** in the ground until you need them, as long as the earth is well drained and cool (cover the rows with straw in a very severe winter). Alternatively, store potatoes in paper sacks and carrots in boxes of sand in a cool, dark, frost-free place. Potatoes, rutabagas, turnips, and beets can also be stored in a clamp: stack the vegetables on a 8 in (20 cm) layer of straw in a pyramid and cover with a layer of longer straw.

- **Onions, shallots, and garlic** will keep all their freshness and potency if hung up in strings, but they need good air circulation to remain in the best condition. They can also be stored in wire baskets if it's difficult to hang them up.

- **Frost-resistant greens** such as cabbages, kale, and Brussels sprouts will neither continue to grow nor fade if left in the ground until you want to eat them.

- **Pumpkins and squashes** should be stored in a well-ventilated place.

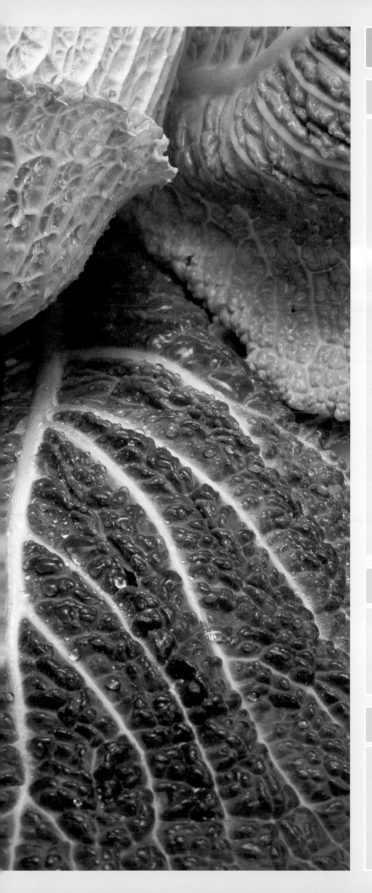

# WINTER PRODUCE

## Vegetables

| | |
|---|---|
| Beets | Kohlrabi |
| Broccoli, purple sprouting | Leeks |
| | Lettuce |
| Brussels sprouts | Onions |
| Cabbages | Parsnips |
| Carrots | Peppers |
| Cauliflowers | Potatoes |
| Celeriac | Pumpkins |
| Celery | Rutabaga |
| Chicory | Salsify |
| Chiles | Squash |
| Garlic | Shallots |
| Jerusalem artichokes | Spinach |
| | Turnips |
| Kale | Watercress |

## Wild produce

| | |
|---|---|
| Sloes | Chestnuts |
| Rosehip | |

## Fruits and nuts

| | |
|---|---|
| Almonds | Rhubarb |
| Pears | Walnuts |

# Pickle vegetables

If you have an abundance of fresh vegetables, pickle some of them in home-made spiced pickling vinegar to preserve them for the Christmas season, or to give away in a gift basket. The pickling process transforms the taste and texture of these fresh vegetables into more complex flavors, which taste good with a variety of different foods such as fish, game, and cold meats.

## Homemade spiced pickling vinegar

- 6 cups (1.14 liters) malt vinegar
- A few pieces of blade mace
- 20 cloves
- 20 whole allspice berries
- 1 cinnamon stick
- 6 peppercorns
- 1 cup raw cane sugar

1. Boil all the ingredients together in a pan for a few minutes. Then cover and leave the liquid for 2 hours to cool completely. Strain into sterilized bottles until needed (p.125).

2. Use preserving jars with vinegar-proof lids when you bottle the vegetables in pickling vinegar. Leave the pickles to mature for at least three months before using them.

Salt, oil, and vinegar all prevent vegetables from decay by protecting them from the bacteria that could rot them. Salt draws out moisture and creates an inhospitable environment for bacteria, oil coats the produce to prevent contamination from the air, and the acid in vinegar, known as acetic acid, inhibits bacterial growth. Pickling combines the preservative qualities of salt and vinegar, and it's an ideal way to preserve vegetables such as beans, cabbage, cauliflower, cucumbers, onions, and shallots. Use the freshest, crispest produce for the best results.

## Brining and potting up

The vegetables need "brining" in salt water first before being preserved in vinegar, to draw out the moisture that would otherwise seep into the vinegar and dilute it. The brining time varies: dense vegetables such as shallots need longer than beans or cucumbers. Use coarse salt, as it contains none of the anti-caking agents that are added to table salt. For 3¼ lb (1.5 kg) of shallots, mix 8 pints (4.5 liters) of water and 1 lb (450 g) salt into a brine, add the shallots, and leave for 12 hours with a plate on top to weigh the shallots down and keep them submerged. Then skin the shallots and cover them with fresh brine for a further 24 hours before placing them in sterilized preserving jars (p.125). Pour over the spiced pickling vinegar (left) to completely cover them, and then seal the jars. As well as preserving the vegetables, this spiced pickling vinegar adds a lovely delicate flavor.

# Source your food locally

There's no guarantee that you'll be buying the freshest, tastiest produce if you shop in a supermarket: the food items on sale may well have traveled thousands of miles. Local producers grow or rear produce for the best flavor and freshness, so it's worth reconsidering how and where you shop.

## Make a resolution

Christmas and New Year are traditionally a time to think about breaking old habits, make new resolutions, and put those good intentions into practice, so Christmas is a perfect time to rethink the way you shop as you prepare for the holiday festivites. Source all your ingredients from diverse, small-scale, local producers that grow and rear their produce for quality, not quantity, and you'll be feeding your family the tastiest, freshest food at its highest nutritional value. They'll also be free from the pesticides and fertilizers that are used on air-freighted produce to control the ripening time, and the hormones and antibiotics commonly used by large-scale commercial meat producers to rear their animals.

## Local benefits

If you initially spend a little time locating and researching your local producers, shopping locally can become as easy and convienient as going to the supermarket. You'll also be supporting your local economy, reducing the environmental impact of imported foods, and helping to sustain food security and variety.

## Fair trade

Perhaps one of the most important benefits of shopping locally is that your support ensures that farmers are paid a fair price for their produce. There are currently no laws protecting farmers from the often unreasonable demands made by some of the larger supermarkets—such as paying prices that don't cover the farmers' growing costs, insisting on perfectly shaped fruits and vegetables at the expense of quality and flavor, and requiring minimum quantities of a particular produce, which can prevent the farmers from diversifying into growing other crops, and which in turn affects the quality of the soil for generations to come.

## Good standards

Most small, specialized producers naturally farm organically even if they are not certified as organic farmers, because they follow traditional farming methods. Small-scale animal husbandry, for instance, avoids the use of large quantities of hormones and antibiotics, which results in healthier, happier animals, and good-quality meat. However, if you want complete assurance about the food you buy, look out for a recognized organic certification (the rules and regulations vary from country to country).

# Where to go for local food

## Producers

The easiest way to shop locally is to find your nearest producer and see if you can buy food direct. By buying straight from the farmer's markets, you are helping the farmers get a fairer price for their produce, and enabling them to continue to strive to produce quality food.

## Farmers' markets

This is by far the most enjoyable, and sociable, way to do your shopping. Often held outdoors, these markets are full of the freshest seasonal produce and the tastiest varieties of fruit and vegetables. You can also chat with the suppliers and find out how they rear or grow their produce, and make informed choices about what you and your family will eat.

## Christmas markets

Famous in mainland Europe, Christmas markets are now growing in popularity in North America. They are a good source for specialized goods.

## Independent shops

The increase of supermarkets has meant that small, independent butchers, fish-sellers, and grocery shops are becoming rarer. Although they are often considered less convenient than a superstore, independent retailers will often give invaluable advice on the produce they have on sale, and can prepare your purchase in exactly the way that you want. All in all, it is a much more personalized way to shop. If you are lucky enough to find a selection of small, specialized shops, do your best to support them by purchasing as much of your food from them as you can.

## Food facts

- **Although the UK** could meet up to 70 percent of its food needs, air-freighting fresh produce has more than trebled in the past 20 years. If present trends continue, we could end up relying on foreign imports for most of our everyday goods.

- **It has been estimated** that we are losing 11 farmers everyday in the UK due to impossible multi-national-imposed working contracts. Without the farmers, there is no food security.

- **According to the University of Manchester**, the ingredients for a typical Christmas dinner in the UK will have traveled a combined distance of 49,000 food miles from producers and growers. Turkeys from Europe, African vegetables, Australian wine, and cranberry sauce from the United States, for example, will have notched up the equivalent of 6,000 car trips around the world.

- **Farmers' market stallholders** are required to have grown, reared, caught, brewed, pickled, baked, made, or smoked the produce they sell within a required radius of the market. This is usually a distance of 30 miles (50 km), but in the case of cities or remote regions it can extend to 50 miles (80 km). A minimum of one major ingredient must be local. The stallholder must be the producer, or directly involved in the production process, so that customers can directly ask questions about the farming and food production employed.

## Box schemes

Once a week, a mixed box of seasonal vegetables and fruit, usually sourced from small local suppliers, is delivered directly to your home. The emphasis is on flavor, quality, and freshness. It's a great way of discovering vegetables that you may never have considered cooking with before, and the unpredictable mix will entice you to be more adventurous with your cooking. Look for local box schemes on the internet, or ask around at your local farmers' market.

# Shortbread cookies

Shortbread is traditionally baked in ceramic molds, or in a round tin and cut into petticoat tails or wedges, but use whatever shaped tray you have to hand for these crisp, yet wonderfully crumbly, cookies. To make festive shortbread shapes, roll the dough out to a thickness of ⅛–¼ in (3–5 mm), cut the shapes with cookie cutters, and bake in the oven for 12–15 minutes.

**1** Grease and flour a baking tray. Cream together the butter and sugar in a bowl until the mix looks pale. Sift and mix in the flour and semolina, a little at a time.

**2** Draw the mixture together with your fingertips to form a dough and tip it out onto a clean, lightly floured surface. Knead the dough to a smooth, uniform consistency.

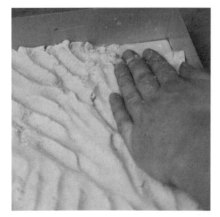

**3** Put the dough into the prepared tray, press it down evenly, and prick it all over with a fork. Sprinkle sugar over the top and chill in the fridge for 15 minutes until firm.

**4** Bake for 30 minutes or until pale brown in color. Leave in the tray for 5 minutes, then slice into fingers, or triangles if you have used round trays, and leave to cool on a wire rack.

## ingredients

**Makes 12 cookies**

Preheat the oven to 300°F (150°C)

- 8 oz (225 g) butter
- ½ cup superfine sugar
- 2¼ cups all-purpose flour
- ¼ cup fine semolina
- A little extra sugar

### 🍃 Cooking tip

**Kneading and freezing** Work quickly and lightly as you knead the shortbread dough: the butter in the mix will soften and turn greasy if you overwork the dough, so the less you handle it, the better it will taste when baked. The cooked cookies can be frozen for up to one month.

# Marshmallow sweets

It's essential that you use a sugar thermometer to achieve the correct boiling point when heating the sugar solution in this recipe. The sugar syrup is extremely dangerous at this high temperature, so take care and keep children well away from the pan. The soft marshmallows keep well for three to four days if stored in an airtight tin lined with baking parchment.

## ingredients

- 2 tbsp confectioner's sugar
- 2 tbsp cornstarch
- 8 sheets leaf gelatine (1 oz/25 g)
- ½ cup hot water
- 2–3 drops organic food coloring (optional)
- 1 lb 1½ oz (500 g) granulated sugar
- 1 cup cold water
- 2 egg whites

### Cooking tip

**Toasting marshmallows**
If children want to toast their marshmallows over an open fire, tie a fork handle securely to one end of a bamboo stick with a piece of string. Push a square of marshmallow onto the prongs of the fork and give the other end of the bamboo stick to the child to hold.

**1** Lightly oil a baking tray. Mix the confectioner's sugar and cornstarch and sift a little into the baking tray to coat it. Dissolve the gelatine in the water in a small bowl.

**2** Put the sugar and water in a large pan, stand a thermometer in the pan and heat the sugar syrup to 252°F (122°C). In the meantime, whisk the egg whites until stiff.

**3** Take the boiling syrup off the heat and mix in the dissolved gelatine. Then gradually beat the syrup into the beaten egg whites. The texture should be thick and creamy.

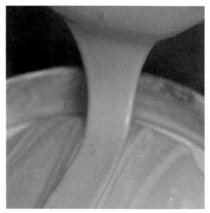

**4** Pour mix into tray and leave to set in a cool place. Once cool, cut into squares. Lightly coat each square in the confectioner's sugar and cornstarch mix. Store in an airtight tin.

# Roasting chestnuts

If you want to roast a handful of chestnuts over an open fire, choose a cast-iron pan, or buy a special roasting pan that has holes punched into the base. For more tips on roasting chestnuts, see page 167.

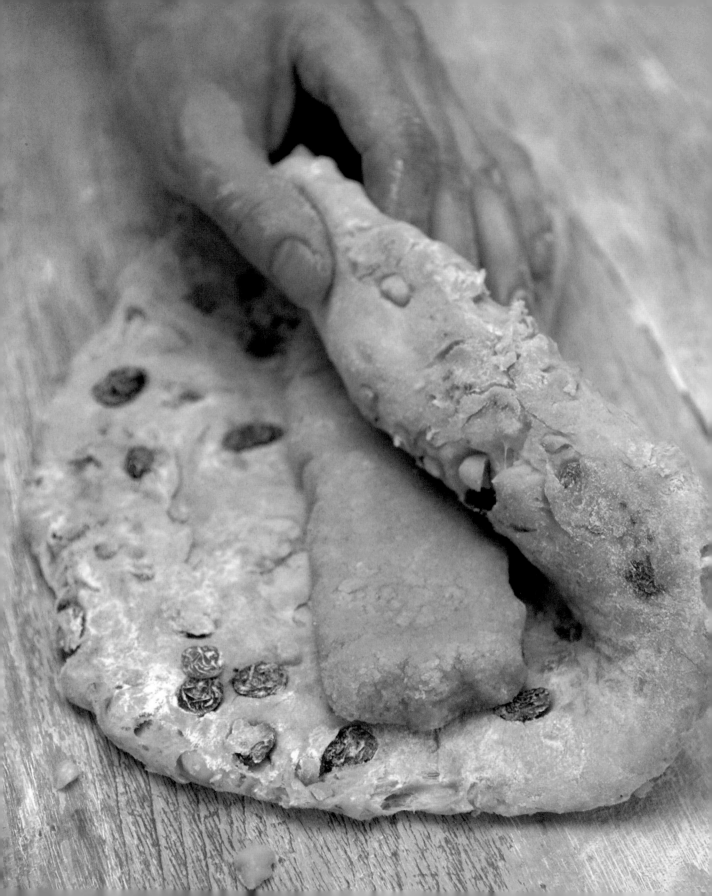

# Stollen

This rich, German Christmas bread is filled with rum-soaked fruits and wrapped around an almond paste center—symbolizing the baby Jesus wrapped in swaddling clothes. The loaf is baked if it sounds hollow when tapped on the base. As you let it cool on a wire rack, brush the top with melted butter, and then dust with confectioner's sugar just before serving it.

**1** Put the golden raisins and currants in a small bowl. Warm rum in a small pan, pour it over the fruits and leave to one side to allow the alcohol to soak into the fruits.

**2** Mix the flour, sugar, and spices, pour in the yeasty milk, and make a batter. Cover with a dry dishcloth and leave in a warm place for half an hour. Then add the butter and egg.

**3** Mix into a dough, knead for 8–10 minutes *(p.226)*, rest for 1–2 hours *(p.230)*, or until doubled in size. Mix the filling ingredients into a paste. Knead all the fruits and nuts into the dough.

**4** Roll the dough into an oval shape. Form the paste into a long roll, put it in the center, fold the dough over the paste, brush the edges with milk, rest for 40–60 minutes, and bake.

## ingredients

Preheat the oven to 400°F (200°C)

Bake for 30 minutes

- ½ cup golden raisins
- ¼ cup currants
- 3 tbsp rum
- 3 cups white flour
- ¼ cup superfine sugar
- ½ tsp ground cardamom
- 1½ tsp ground cinnamon
- 2 tsp dried yeast mixed with ¾ cup lukewarm milk
- 4 tbsp butter, melted
- 1 egg, lightly beaten
- ¼ cup chopped candied citron
- ½ cup almonds, chopped

**For the almond filling**

- ¾ cup finely ground almonds
- ¼ cup superfine sugar
- 1 cup confectioner's sugar
- 1½ tsp lemon juice
- ½ egg, lightly beaten

# Honey-roast ham

Use a cured ham with the skin on; boiling the ham will loosen the skin. The skin should be removed before roasting, exposing the fat layer, which should be scored. If you serve this ham hot for one meal, use the cold meat in salads, sandwiches, and soups—it will keep well for a good seven days in the fridge.

## ingredients

Preheat the oven to 350°F (180°C)

- 6½ lb (3 kg) organic cured ham with the skin
- 2 sticks celery, coarsely chopped
- 2 carrots, coarsely chopped
- 1 onion, coarsely chopped
- 8 black peppercorns, 2 bay leaves, 4 sprigs thyme, a few fresh parsley stems, and 12–16 cloves all wrapped up in a sachet (p.175)
- A handful of extra cloves
- 4 tbsp honey
- 1½ tbsp English mustard

**1** Place the ham, vegetables, and sachet in a pan. Cover with cold water. Bring to the boil, and then simmer for 1¾ hours. Then lift the ham on to a board and cut away the skin.

**2** A smooth layer of fat should be left on the ham. Score the fat with a sharp knife, first in one direction and then in the opposite direction, to make a diamond pattern.

**3** Stud the fat with cloves: place a clove at the center of each diamond shape. Transfer the ham to a metal roasting tray. Mix together the honey and mustard for the glaze.

**4** Drizzle the glaze evenly over the fat. Roast in the pre-heated oven for about 45 minutes, basting with the glaze a couple of times, until the glaze is dark golden. Serve, or leave to cool.

# Spiced nuts

These coated nuts make a crunchy, very tasty homemade snack that is a tasty change from ordinary nuts and chips. If you prefer, you can substitute the spices for either cumin seeds, sesame seeds, nigella seeds, or a few chile flakes. Store any leftover nuts in an airtight jar and consume them within three days.

**1** Remove all the shells, if you have bought unshelled nuts, and finely chop the rosemary leaves (discard the tough stalks).

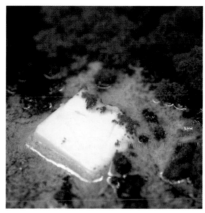

**2** Melt the butter and sugar in a large, heavy saucepan or frying pan on a low heat. Add the chopped rosemary, cayenne pepper, paprika, and salt and then toss in the nuts.

**3** Stir until the nuts are evenly coated with the spice mix. Toast on a low heat, stirring or tossing frequently until the coated nuts look golden brown and crisp.

**4** Tip the nuts onto a large sheet of wax paper, arrange in a single layer, and leave to cool before serving in small bowls.

## ingredients

**serves six to eight people**

- 10½ oz (300 g) mixed unsalted nuts
- A few sprigs of fresh rosemary
- 3 tbsp unsalted butter
- 2 tbsp soft dark brown sugar
- ½ tsp cayenne pepper
- 2 tsp mild Spanish paprika
- A good pinch of sea salt

# Parsnip crisps

For a delicious, instant snack, shave a few parsnips with a vegetable peeler to create thin strips, shallow-fry them briefly in oil in a heavy saucepan, lift them out, drain off the oil, and sprinkle with salt.

# Make mulled drinks

Winter is the time to enjoy warming drinks to keep the chilly weather at bay. Mulled drinks have long been part of our winter traditions: mead—a fermented drink made of honey, water, and yeast—was flavored with spices and sometimes fruits, and heated by plunging a hot poker into the liquid; and wassail, a hot, spiced punch often associated with winter celebrations in northern Europe, derives from medieval times, when it was more like a mulled beer seasoned with spices and honey. These drinks are easy to prepare and taste delicious.

Mulled wine can be left warming on the stove all evening, but don't let it boil or the alcohol will evaporate. If you want to prepare it ahead of time, heat the wine, spices, lemon rind, sugar, and the orange studded with cloves to simmering point, turn off the heat, and leave to marinate for a few hours before adding the orange juice, brandy, and orange slices.

## Mulled wine

Pour 2 bottles of red wine into a large pan and add 1 orange studded with 12 cloves, the pared zest of 1 lemon, a 2 in (5 cm) piece of fresh ginger, peeled and cut into slices, 2 cinnamon sticks, 4 tablespoons of brandy, ½ cup demerara sugar, the juice of 1 orange, and 1 thinly sliced orange. Bring almost to the boil on a medium heat, stirring until the sugar has dissolved. Turn the heat down and simmer for 30 minutes, then serve in glasses.

## Hot pear cup

Cut ½ a crisp apple into slices and stud each slice with a couple of cloves. Place the slices in a large pan, add 3½ cups pear cider, 1 vanilla bean, 1 large piece of pared lemon zest, ⅔ cup brandy, 1 cinnamon stick, 2 tablespoons of honey, and bring to the boil. Simmer gently for 10 minutes, then serve in four glasses.

## Winter whiskey sour

Stud 4 lemon slices with 3 cloves each. Place in a pan with 1 strip of lemon rind, 2 tablespoons of maple syrup, and 1¾ cups water. Bring to the boil, then turn off the heat and leave to infuse for 5 minutes. Divide a ½ cup whiskey and the 4 lemon slices between 4 glasses, discard the lemon rind, add the infused water, and serve.

# Choose a Christmas bird

If you love to eat a traditional Christmas dinner of roast turkey, goose, or chicken, there's every reason to source the best-quality meat possible for your meal. The freshness and flavor of a locally produced organic or free-range bird just can't be beaten, so buy from a supplier or producer you know and trust.

## Poultry farming

Since the advent of industry farming and breeding technology in the twentieth century, commercial poultry farmers have been able to produce bigger birds in a restricted environment in a shorter space of time. The impact of these intensive farming methods has meant that the amount of cheap meat now available has increased dramatically.

Recently, however, the trend in farming has begun to shift back towards smaller-scale poultry farmers using traditional, more holistic ways of rearing their flocks to provide good-quality, flavorsome birds.

## Organic and free-range

Organic and free-range birds are kept in smaller groups than conventional poultry, in spaces large enough for them to move around freely and have access to open pastures and water. As a result, the birds have longer, happier, less stressful lives. The smaller groups establish a natural pecking order that helps to allay the aggression and attacks that often occur between confined birds. These birds are fed on a nutritious, balanced diet.

Organic turkeys may be smaller that their commercial counterparts, but because they live longer, the meat will have more flavor. Geese are grazing birds, and the better the grass, the better the end result. The geese are fed a cereal-based diet until they are about 12 weeks old, and then again once the nutrients in grass decrease in wintertime. Sometimes, the only difference between organic and free-range birds is the type of feed used. Organic feed can be costly for a smallholder, as can the organic certification.

## The provenance of poultry

Knowing who you are buying your food from will make all the difference to the quality of your meat. It's worth finding a reliable local supplier and asking them how the birds have been reared and killed, and what type of feed has been used – or contact the farmer direct to get answers to your questions. If you can visit the farm to make your order, you may even be able to see the birds in their environment. Small-scale producers are passionate about their food, and work hard to make sure their produce tastes as good as it can on your plate. So your carefully chosen bird should end up as a fabulously tasty meal.

# Product labels

If you choose to shop for chicken or other poultry in a supermarket, it's important to check the various labels and understand what they mean in order to make sure that you buy well-reared poultry:

**Standard** (carries a red tractor logo)
Up to 10,000 turkeys and 50,000 chickens at a time are kept in windowless, airless sheds, which is about 17 chickens per square meter, or the equivalent of each bird living in a space the size of an letter-sized sheet of paper. Lighting is kept dim to discourage bird activity, and the sheds are dark for only one hour in every five to encourage the birds to keep eating. There are no perches or toys to distract the birds from eating, and they are fed a high-protein cereal diet so that they quickly put on weight. The average age of these chickens at slaughter is 37 to 40 days.

**Freedom food barn-reared**
These birds are reared in sheds, but at lower stocking densities (for chickens, it is the equivalent size of 1.25 sheets of letter-sized paper per bird). Lighting is varied to simulate night and day: six hours of darkness at night allows the birds to rest properly. Perches, straw bales, and toys encourage birds to peck and be active. The birds are corn-fed, so they grow more slowly, have lower mortality rates, and are less likely to suffer leg and hip problems, hock burn, and foot pad burn. The average age of these chickens at slaughter is 50 days.

## Poultry farming facts

- **Ten million turkeys** are bred every year for Christmas consumption in the UK, mostly in dark, cramped conditions.

- **Forty years ago**, it took 84 days for a broiler chicken to reach market weight; now, it can take as little as 37 days to achieve the same weight.

- **Broiler chickens** typically have a splayed gait and pronounced waddle—a result of leg and hip injuries caused by their accelerated development. They also suffer obesity and heart disease from such rapid weight gain, and hock, breast, and foot-pad burn from constantly sitting in soiled litter.

- **Some commercially reared** giant turkeys can be reared to weigh almost 88 lb (40 kg) in just 30 weeks. By comparison, an adult organic turkey such as a KellyBronze will only weigh about 10–11 lb (5 kg) at the same age (KellyBronze birds are over six months old when they are killed).

## Free-range

Smaller stocks of birds are housed in sheds and have free access to the outdoors during daylight. These birds have a more varied diet: cereal feed, plus grass, seeds, and clover. Due to their outdoor life, the birds have fewer leg and hip injuries, and good muscle development. The average age of these chickens at slaughter is 56 days.

## Organic

Small flocks of up to 1,000 birds roam outdoors during the day on land planted with vegetation, and at night in small huts that are occasionally moved around to let the land rest. The birds have a longer, healthier outdoor life with a natural diet of organic cereal feed, grass, seeds, and clover. The average age of these chickens at slaughter is 81 days.

# Edible display

A bowl of fruit makes a natural and unfussy decorative centerpiece for a table; find a large, rustic-looking bowl and fill it with generous quantities of seasonal fruits such as apples and pears.

# Roast a bird

A good Christmas dinner is all about choosing the best ingredients and cooking them well. Whether you cook a goose, turkey, or a chicken, choose quality over quantity, and provide plenty of vegetables to make the meal go further. Follow these simple guidelines for a succulent, perfectly cooked bird.

## Storing the bird

Once you've ordered your bird, collect it three to five days before the planned meal. Ask your butcher to take off the legs and neck if necessary, then keep it unwrapped in a very cool cabinet or in the fridge. When you want to roast the bird, remove it from the fridge, wash it, pat it dry, and leave it for at least two hours to come to room temperature before cooking it.

## Preparing a turkey or chicken

Place the bird in a roasting pan and rub the skin with salt and pepper, or mix a little softened butter, crushed garlic, lemon zest, chopped fresh rosemary and thyme, and black pepper. Lift the skin away from the flesh, smear the butter under the skin and over the breast, and then re-cover the flesh with the skin. Preheat the oven and calculate the cooking time according to the weight of the bird.

## Preparing a goose

Place the bird on a wire tray over a roasting pan, remove any excess fat from inside the cavity of the goose, and season it inside and out with salt and pepper. Alternatively, put a couple of fresh sprigs of thyme and rosemary and a whole bulb of garlic into the cavity, along with half a teacup of water. Prick the fat gland under the wings of the goose and around the back by the "parson's nose." If the legs are still attached, rub them with a little butter or cooking oil and cover them with kitchen foil to prevent them burning. Preheat the oven and calculate the cooking time according to the weight of the bird.

## Cooking the bird

Cook the stuffing separately so that hot air can circulate in the main cavity of the bird. This helps to reduce the cooking time and produces more succulent meat. It also means that the breast meat doesn't overcook.

The bird is cooked if the juices run clear when a sharp knife is inserted into the flesh. Cover it loosely with kitchen foil and clean dishcloths and leave it in a warm place away from draughts to rest for 30–60 minutes to allow the juices to soak back into the meat and make it more succulent. Just before the bird is ready to be served, warm the plates and dishes.

## Make a tasty stock

- 1 small whole chicken (ask your butcher to remove the breasts first), or a raw carcass, if your butcher has one
- 2 celery stalks, sliced
- 2 large carrots, sliced
- 1 leek sliced
- ½ parsnip, sliced
- 1 large onion, peeled and sliced
- 1 potato, diced
- ¼ rutabaga, sliced
- A little salt
- 5¼ pints (3 liters) boiling water

1. Place the chicken and all the vegetables in a large stockpot. Season with a little salt, add the boiling water, and cover with a lid.

2. Bring back to a boil and allow to boil for 5 minutes. Then cover the pot, lower the heat and leave to simmer for 2 hours.

3. Pour the entire contents of the pot through a sieve with a large enough bowl beneath it to collect all the stock. Leave the stock to cool, then skim any fat off the surface.

4. Discard the vegetables, chicken bones, and skin that remain in the sieve. The stock can be stored in the fridge for a day or so until you need to use it, or frozen for up to a month.

## Make a good gravy

- 1 tbsp oil
- 1 tbsp butter
- 1 large onion, chopped
- 4 cloves garlic, crushed
- 1 tsp redcurrant jelly
- 2 tbsp all-purpose flour
- 1 tsp tomato purée
- 3 cups chicken stock
- 3 sprigs fresh thyme, leaves removed and chopped
- Salt and pepper
- Good glug of red wine

1. Heat the oil and butter in a heavy-bottomed pan. Add the onion, garlic, and redcurrant jelly and cook slowly on a low heat, stirring occasionally, for about 30 minutes, until the onions are brown and caramelized.

2. Stir in the flour and tomato purée and allow to cook for a minute before slowly pouring in the stock, stirring continually. Add the thyme, seasoning, and the red wine. Alternatively, the red wine can be replaced with white wine, sherry, or cider.

3. A really good gravy needs the addition of meat juices. If you are roasting meat or poultry, pour off any excess fat from the roasting pan, deglaze it with a little stock or wine, and add the liquid to the gravy.

4. Cover and simmer gently for 10 minutes, stirring occasionally, then serve with the bird.

# Cranberry jelly

This tart, fruity preserve is not only perfect with a roast turkey or chicken on Christmas day, but it also complements pork, sausages and any cold meats you may serve over the festive season. Store the jars in a pantry or a cool, dark cabinet for up to one year. Once opened, a jar of jelly should keep well in the fridge for up to three weeks.

**1** Check the cranberries and discard any that have brown spots or are shriveled. Put the berries and water in a saucepan and bring to the boil over a medium heat.

**2** Turn the heat down and simmer the mixture until the cranberries are tender. Then place a fine sieve over a bowl and pour the cranberry mixture into the sieve.

**3** Press the berries through the sieve with a spoon to produce a smooth pulp in the bowl. Return the pulp and juice to the saucepan, bring to the boil, and add the sugar.

**4** Allow the mix to simmer for 10 minutes, then test for the setting point *(p.132)*. If the jelly sets when tested, pour into sterilized jars *(p.132)*, seal, label, and date the jars.

## ingredients

**Makes about 2 cups of jelly**

- 1 lb (450 g) fresh cranberries
- 1½ cups water
- 1 lb (450 g) superfine sugar

### 🍃 Cooking tip

**Frozen cranberries**
If you find it hard to find fresh cranberries, a bag of frozen fruits will work just as well for this recipe (avoid dried cranberries). There's no need to thaw the berries first before you cook them.

# Make a stuffing

A good, tasty stuffing packed with flavorsome ingredients and plenty of fresh herbs will always enhance a classic holiday dinner beautifully, but it needn't just be an accompaniment for meat. A stuffing served with a vegetarian main dish will also make for an equally delicious meal.

## Herb and pine nut

- 4 oz (110 g) butter
- 1 onion, finely chopped
- 1 garlic clove, crushed
- 1 large sprig thyme, leaves only
- 1 large sprig rosemary, leaves chopped
- 6 fresh sage leaves, chopped
- 3 packed cups fresh white breadcrumbs
- Zest of 1 lemon
- ½ cup pine nuts
- Salt and pepper
- 3 tbsp fresh parsley, chopped

1. Melt the butter in a pan and gently sauté the onion and garlic until soft. Stir in the herbs and cook for one minute. Then add the breadcrumbs and let them absorb the butter in the pan.

2. Mix in the zest, pine nuts, and seasoning and cook on a medium to high heat until the crumbs start to brown and turn crisp.

3. Remove from the heat, stir in the parsley, and serve.

## Thyme and parsley

- 1 large onion, finely chopped
- 1 stick butter, plus more as needed
- 3 packed cups fresh white breadcrumbs
- 2 tsp lemon thyme leaves
- 2 tbsp fresh parsley, chopped
- Zest of 1 lemon
- Salt and pepper
- 1 tbsp milk

1. Preheat the oven to 350°F (180°C).

2. Sweat the onion gently in the butter in a saucepan on a low to medium heat until soft.

3. Mix the breadcrumbs, herbs, and lemon zest in a bowl, then add the sweated onions. Season well and stir in enough milk to bind the mixture together.

4. Place in an ovenproof dish, dot with a little extra butter and bake in the oven for approximately 30 minutes, or until golden brown and firm to the touch.

# Apricot and cumin

- ¾ cup dried apricots, soaked overnight and drained
- ⅓ cup pine nuts, toasted
- 1 cup fresh white breadcrumbs
- 1 tbsp olive oil
- 1 tbsp cumin seeds, toasted and ground in a pestle and mortar
- Salt and pepper
- Extra breadcrumbs for covering the stuffing balls

1. Finely chop the apricots and pine nuts (or pulse them to a rough paste in a food processor).

2. Put them into a bowl and mix in the breadcrumbs, olive oil, cumin, salt, and pepper. Leave to stand for a few minutes.

3. Form the stuffing into approximately 12 balls, roll each one in the extra breadcrumbs and roast in the oven on a baking tray, or around the roast, at about 375°F (190°C) for 25 minutes.

4. If you wish, you can add 9 oz (250 g) of cooked sausage meat when you add the breadcrumbs. This increased quantity will make about 20 balls of stuffing.

# Sage, onion, and smoked bacon

- 1 onion, finely chopped
- 3 strips organic or free-range smoked bacon, chopped
- 1 tbsp olive oil
- 2 tbsp butter
- 1 cup fresh white breadcrumbs
- 1 heaped tbsp chopped fresh sage
- Salt and pepper
- 1 medium egg, lightly beaten
- A little fresh parsley, chopped

1. Cook the onion and bacon in the oil in a saucepan on a medium heat until the bacon is just beginning to brown.

2. Melt the butter, then add breadcrumbs and sage and season well. Stir in the beaten egg to bind the mixture together.

3. Place the stuffing in an ovenproof dish and bake in the oven at 180°C (350°F/Gas 4) for approximately 30 minutes, or until the stuffing is golden brown and firm to touch. Scatter the chopped fresh parsley over the stuffing just before serving it.

4. If you wish, you can also add 9oz (250 g) of cooked sausage meat when you add the breadcrumbs.

# Chocolate log

Known as a *Bûche de Noel* in France, this chocolate cake can be served as a dessert, or with coffee. Bake the sponge in advance if you need to prepare ahead; to keep it moist, wet some wax paper, wring it out, wrap it around the cooled sponge, and put the cake in a plastic bag. This will keep it fresh for a day or so until you are ready to roll and decorate it.

## ingredients

Preheat the oven to 400°F (200°C)

**For the sponge**
- 4 extra-large eggs at room temperature
- ½ cup superfine sugar
- ½ cup self-rising flour
- ¼ cup cocoa powder

**For the filling**
- 8 oz (225 g) can unsweetened chestnut purée
- 1 tbsp coffee extract
- ¼ cup superfine sugar
- ½ cup plus 2 tbsp heavy cream, stiffly whipped
- 2 tbsp brandy

**For the fudge icing**
- 4 tbsp melted butter
- 3 tbsp cocoa powder
- About 3 tbsp milk
- 1 cup confectioner's sugar, sifted

**1** Grease and line a jelly roll pan. Whisk together the eggs and sugar in a large bowl until the mix is light, then sift in the flour and cocoa and fold them into the mixture.

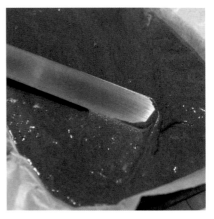

**2** Turn the mix into the prepared pan and spread it evenly. Bake in a preheated oven for 10 minutes. Turn the cake out onto wax paper and leave to cool.

**3** To make the filling, put the purée in a bowl and beat in the coffee extract and sugar until smooth. Fold in the cream and brandy. Spread the filling over the cooled sponge.

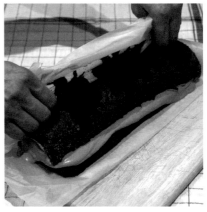

**4** Peel off the paper as you roll the sponge up. Mix the butter and cocoa, add the milk and confectioner's sugar, beat until smooth. Decorate the cake to look like a log.

# Bake a ginger cake

It's worth making this deliciously moist cake at least two or three days before you want to serve it: the cake will store well in an airtight tin and, as the days go by, it will mature in flavor—if it lasts that long! Serve individual portions of the cake with a small spoonful of whipped cream or crème fraîche on the side.

**1** Grease and line a round 9¾ in (25 cm) cake tin with parchment paper. Put the syrup, molasses, butter and sugar in a saucepan and bring gently to the boil.

**2** Put the measured flour, spices and baking soda into a large bowl and add the melted ingredients.

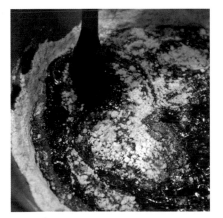

**3** Mix the dry and the melted ingredients together well with a wooden spoon. Add the beaten eggs and mix thoroughly, then add the boiling water.

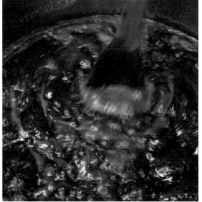

**4** Combine all the ingredients thoroughly. Pour the mix into the lined tin. Cook for 45–50 minutes, or until the cake springs back if pressed lightly. Leave to cool in the tin.

## ingredients

Preheat the oven to 350°F (180°C)

- 1 cup sugar syrup
- 1 cup molasses
- 2 sticks butter
- 3 cups superfine sugar
- 3 cups all-purpose flour, sifted
- 1–2 tsp ground ginger
- 1 tsp pumpkin pie spice
- 1 tsp baking soda
- 2 large eggs
- 6fl oz (170 ml) boiling water

# Mini panettone

This sweet Italian Christmas bread is rich in butter, eggs, and dried fruits, yet it is deliciously light and soft. Italians traditionally have a slice of panettone with a glass of Champagne on Christmas day. Avoid leaving any dried fruit on the surface of the dough as you put it into the molds, or it will burn in the oven and turn hard and bitter.

## ingredients

**Makes 12 mini loaves**

Preheat the oven to 180°C (350°F)

Bake for 20 minutes

- 12 mini pudding molds, greased
- 18 oz (500 g) unbleached white bread flour
- ½ tsp salt
- 1 tsp dried yeast
- ½ cup lukewarm milk
- 2 eggs
- 2 egg yolks
- 10 tbsp butter, softened
- ¼ cup plus 2 tbsp superfine sugar
- ¼ cup mixed candied citron
- ½ cup raisins
- Melted butter for brushing

**1** Sift the flour into a bowl, add the salt, and make a well. Whisk the yeast, milk, and eggs together, pour into the well, mix in a little flour to make a batter, and rest for 30 minutes *(p.230)*.

**2** Add the egg yolks, softened butter, and sugar and mix them and the rest of the flour into the batter with a fork. Then bind the ingredients together into a ball with your hands.

**3** Knead the dough for 5 minutes *(p.226)* and leave to rest in a warm, but not too warm, place for 1½–2 hours, or until doubled in size. Then scatter over the peel and raisins.

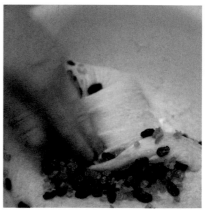

**4** Gently knead in the peel and the raisins. Divide into 12, place in the molds, cover with a dry dishcloth, and rest for 1 hour. Then brush the tops with melted butter and bake.

# Reuse your leftovers

If you feel apprehensive about serving cold meats or leftover desserts for several more meals after the main event, or if you've over-cooked and have extra supplies of vegetables that you're thinking of throwing away, try these simple solutions to using up Christmas leftovers.

## Parsnip and apple soup

**Serves six to eight people**

- 2 leeks, washed and sliced
- 1 medium onion, diced
- 2 carrots, peeled and diced
- 2 celery sticks
- 2 garlic cloves, peeled and sliced
- 6–8 leftover cooked parsnips or 3 raw parsnips, diced
- 3 apples, peeled and cored
- 6 cups chicken stock
- 1 tsp cinnamon (optional)
- Salt and pepper
- 4 tbsp heavy cream (optional)

1. Place the leeks, onion, carrots, celery, and garlic into a saucepan and cook them until soft, but without taking on any color.

2. Add the parsnips and apples and cook for 2 minutes. Add the stock and bring to the boil. Simmer until the vegetables are tender, then add the cinnamon, if you wish.

3. Using a hand blender, blitz the soup until smooth. Adjust the seasoning, add the cream if you wish, and serve.

## Pea and ham soup

**Serves six to eight people**

- 1 tbsp olive oil
- 1 tbsp butter
- 2 leeks, washed and sliced
- 1 medium onion, diced
- 2 carrots, peeled and diced
- 2 celery sticks, thinly sliced
- 2 garlic cloves, peeled and sliced
- 1½ cups ham, diced
- 3½ cups chicken stock
- Salt and pepper
- 1 x 14 oz (400 g) bag frozen peas

1. Heat the oil and butter in a large saucepan. Add the leeks, onion, carrots, celery, and garlic and cook them until soft, but not taking on any color.

2. Add the ham, stock, and seasoning and simmer for 10 minutes. Add the peas, bring the soup back to the boil and simmer for 5 minutes or so.

3. Using a hand blender, pulse the mixture until the soup has a lovely rich, coarse texture. Adjust the seasoning and serve.

# Winter pilaf

**Serves two as a main course with Indian chutneys, or four to six as a side dish**

- 1 medium onion, peeled and sliced
- 2 garlic cloves, peeled and thinly sliced
- 1 tbsp oil
- 1 tsp cumin
- 1½ tsp garam masala
- Dried chile flakes—you choose how much
- 1 mug basmati rice
- Approx 1½ mugs chicken stock
- A small handful golden raisins or raisins (optional)
- Some leftover chicken or turkey meat
- ½ mug peas (leftover or frozen)
- Salt and pepper
- A pat of butter
- A few toasted almonds or cashews (optional)
- Fresh cilantro, chopped (optional)

1. Quickly fry the onion and garlic in the oil in a pan on a low to medium heat until soft, then add the spices and fry them for a minute. Add the rice and fry for a minute, stirring all the time. Add enough stock to the pan so that it comes to a fingernail depth above the rice.

2. Add the golden raisins or raisins and the chicken, and peas. Bring to the boil, then reduce the heat so that the stock is simmering. Add the seasoning and a good pat of butter, give it a stir and put on the lid.

3. Simmer for 10–15 minutes. There should be no liquid left in the pan once the rice is cooked. Scatter over toasted nuts and fresh cilantro.

# Bread and butter panettone

**Serves two to four people**

Preheat the oven to 350°F (180°C)

- 1 pint (600 ml) milk
- 1 vanilla bean, split and scraped, and its seeds
- 4 egg yolks
- 4 tsp cornstarch
- 3 tbsp sugar
- 7 oz (200 g) leftover panettone
- 4 tbsp butter
- ¾ cup golden raisins
- 2 tbsp demerara sugar

1. Place the milk in a saucepan with the vanilla beans and pod. Heat on a medium heat until the milk begins to simmer, then remove from the heat and allow the mixture to cool so the vanilla infuses in the milk. In a separate bowl, mix together the egg yolks, cornstarch, and sugar.

2. Bring the vanilla milk back to the boil and pour it over the egg mixture. Then pour all the ingredients back into the saucepan. Put the saucepan back on the heat and stir until the custard begins to thicken. Remove the pan from the heat and allow the custard to cool. Cut the panettone into slices and spread each slice with a little butter.

3. Place the panettone slices evenly in an ovenproof dish, scattering the golden raisins between the layers as you work. Pour the custard over the panettone and bake for 30 minutes, or until the custard has set. Serve immediately.

# Sachertorte

This classic Viennese dark chocolate cake is one of the world's most renowned grown-up cakes. It's quite dense and rich, and not overly sweet, so ideally it should be served in small slices with a little unsweetened whipped cream on the side, accompanied by a cup of coffee or tea. The sachertorte will improve in flavor if you make it a day or so before you want to eat it.

**1** Grease and line a round cake pan (p.242). Beat the butter in a large bowl or mixer until it is really soft. Meanwhile, melt the chocolate in a double boiler (p.126).

**2** Add the sugar to the butter and beat until the mixture is really light and fluffy. Add the vanilla extract and mix well. In a separate bowl, whisk egg whites until stiff.

**3** Add the melted chocolate to the mix, then the egg yolks, one at a time, and the ground almonds and flour. Add about one third of the egg whites and stir well.

**4** Fold in the remaining egg whites, pour into the pan and bake. Once the cake is cool, brush the jam thinly over the surface, spread the chocolate and cream mix on top, and chill.

## ingredients

Preheat the oven to 350°F (180°C)

Bake for 35 minutes

- 5 oz (150 g) unsalted butter, softened
- ½ cup fine sugar
- ½ tsp vanilla extract
- 5 oz (150 g) bittersweet chocolate, broken into pieces
- 5 large eggs, separated, with the whites put into a large bowl
- ⅔ cup ground almonds
- 1⅓ cups all-purpose flour

### For the topping

- 4 tbsp apricot jam, melted
- 5 oz (150 g) bittersweet chocolate, melted in a double boiler and then mixed with 3¼ cups plus 2 tbsp double cream

# Preserved lemons

If lemons are salted and left to cure in a jar, the rind turns into a rich, rounded flavor that adds a marvelously distinctive Middle-Eastern flavor to dishes. Chop the rind and rub it with garlic over a chicken or leg of lamb before roasting, mix it with roasted onions, garlic, and pumpkin pieces, some cooked couscous, raisins, pine nuts, and a stick of cinnamon, or add it to slow-cooked casserole dishes.

## ingredients

These quantities are approximate, but should fill a 3.5-cup (1-liter) jar; adjust the quantities accordingly

- 5 unwaxed organic lemons
- 1 lb 1½ oz (500 g) coarse sea salt
- 2 cinnamon sticks (optional)
- 1 tbsp coriander seeds (optional)
- 1 tbsp whole cumin seeds (optional)
- 1 tsp black peppercorns
- 1 tsp cloves (optional)
- 3 dried red chiles (optional)
- Dried bay leaves
- Enough freshly squeezed lemon juice to cover the contents of the jar

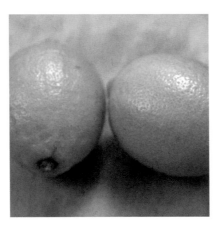

**1** Sterilize the preserving jar (p.125). Wipe the lemons to remove any dirt.

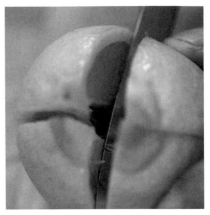

**2** Cut two thirds of the way through each lemon with a sharp knife, then again at right angles to the first cut.

**3** Open out the top of each lemon slightly, fill the cuts with salt, and press the top of each lemon together again. Put a couple of lemons in the jar and pack the salt in around them.

**4** Fill jar with the salt, lemons, spices, and bay leaves. Cover with the lemon juice and seal. Leave for at least two months while the salt slowly dissolves to create a clear liquid.

# Chocolate brittle

A tower of chocolate brittle makes an impressive end to a good meal. This recipe is so simple that you can quickly make up extra quantities if you have supplies in the pantry. For the best-tasting brittle, buy milk and dark chocolate with a high cocoa content, and toast the nuts first in a heavy-based pan over a low heat, shaking them frequently until they are lightly browned.

**1** Make each type of chocolate brittle separately. Break the chocolate slabs into small pieces and place them in a small bowl.

**2** Melt the chocolate slowly in a double boiler (p.126). Stir gently with a spoon every so often to make sure all the chocolate pieces melt.

**3** Lift the bowl of melted chocolate from the saucepan of water and mix in the dry ingredients. Line a baking tray with some parchment paper or plastic wrap.

**4** Pour the mix into the tray. Allow to cool. Refrigerate until solid. Just before serving, turn out onto a board, remove the parchment, and break into chunks with the tip of a knife.

## ingredients

**For the white chocolate brittle**
- 11 oz (300 g) organic white chocolate
- 5½ oz (150 g) macadamia nuts

**For the milk chocolate brittle**
- 11 oz (300 g) organic milk chocolate
- 3½ oz (100 g) hazelnuts
- 3½ oz (100 g) raisins

**For the dark chocolate brittle**
- 11 oz (300 g) organic bittersweet chocolate
- 3½ oz (100 g) pecans
- 3½ oz (100 g) dried cranberries

# Plum pudding

Early November is an ideal time to make a plum pudding, as its flavor matures and improves with age. Plum puddings are traditionally set alight before being served: heat a saucepan, add two tablespoons of brandy, immediately light the brandy with a match, pour it over the pudding, and serve. This quantity makes three 3lb (1¼ liter) puddings, which must be steamed for a total of eight hours.

## ingredients

- 1 cup self-rising flour
- 1 tsp grated nutmeg
- 1½ tsp pumpkin pie spice
- 1 tsp ground cinnamon
- 6 packed cups fresh white breadcrumbs
- 10 oz (280 g) lard
- ½ cup dark brown sugar
- 1 lb (450 g) currants
- 2 lb (900 g) raisins
- 1 lb (450 g) golden raisins
- ½ cup candied citron
- ½ cup sliced almonds
- 1 large cooking apple, grated
- 1 carrot, grated
- 6 eggs
- Juice and zest of 1 orange
- 2 cups stout, ale, or milk
- A little brandy for lighting the pudding

**1** Sift the flour and spices into a large bowl. Add all the remaining dry ingredients and the apple and carrot, and mix well.

**2** Mix the eggs into the mixture, one at a time, then add the orange juice and rind and stir well.

**3** Add the stout, ale, or milk and mix thoroughly. Cut three circles of wax paper that will fit inside the rims of the pudding basins, then butter the insides of the basins.

**4** Decant the mix into the basins, packing it down. Cover with the paper and some tin foil, and secure with string tied into a handle. Steam in stages of two hours, if you wish.

# Compost kitchen waste

We eat more, and create more food waste, during Christmas than at any other time of year. Although it's becoming easier to recycle food and beverage packaging, most of our domestic waste still goes into the trash. Reduce the amount of garbage you throw away by composting your kitchen food waste.

## Undecomposed waste

Food waste sealed in a plastic bag on a landfill site doesn't decompose properly. Instead, it produces methane, a greenhouse gas, which contributes to global warming, and a liquid, leachate, which can contaminate water supplies.

Composting your kitchen food waste is easy and requires little time, effort, or space, depending on which system you use. The compost is invaluable for the soil in your garden or potted plants: it's a complete and natural food for the soil, helping to improve its structure, water-retaining abilities, and overall health.

## Start a wormery

A wormery is small enough to keep on a balcony, patio, or in a porch, so it's ideal if you don't have much outside space. It's also one of the cleanest, neatest, and easiest composting systems to use. A ready-made kit provides both the bin with its lid and the worms; as you fill each layer with small amounts of scraps and leftovers, the worms work their way up through the layers, eating the waste (they consume up to half of their body weight a day). It's this action that speeds up the composting process, leaving you with rich, dark compost in the lowest tray after only a few months. After you've emptied out the compost, the empty tray can be placed on top of the stack and filled with more food waste. The liquid that collects at the bottom of the bin should be siphoned off regularly, but it makes a wonderful tonic for your plants when diluted 1:10 with water. Store it in screw-top wine bottles until you need to use it.

If you regularly add a few handfuls of chopped food waste and shredded dry fiber (cardboard is best), ensure good air circulation, a fairly constant temperature and prevent waterlogging, this efficient composting system should last for years.

### The best waste for a wormery

- Raw or cooked fruit and vegetable peelings
- Pasta, rice, and bread
- Dried and crushed egg shells
- Teabags and coffee grounds
- Dry fiber, such as torn-up egg boxes and empty toilet rolls, to make up 25 percent of the contents

Avoid citrus fruit and onion peelings (which cause acidic conditions), plant seeds, meat, fish, dairy products, dog and cat droppings, spent tissues, grass cuttings and leaves, diseased plant material, and anything in excess.

# Conventional composting

You can recycle both kitchen and garden waste if you keep a compost heap or bin in your garden. An insulating box or bin is essential: make your own from pieces of wood, or buy a ready-made wooden or recycled plastic version. A lid or covering, such as a piece of old carpet, keeps the contents of the bin warm and the rain out. Position the bin on an area of soil so that composting creatures such as worms and soil micro-organisms can help to break down the organic waste in the bin. If you want to "pre-compost" your food waste and accelerate the composting process, add Bokashi active bran to the food waste and leave it to "pickle" for two weeks in a bucket before adding it to the compost bin.

Kitchen waste is high in moisture and has very little structure once it has decomposed. Add a supply of dry material, such as cardboard, scrunched-up paper, coarse twigs, and stems to stop the compost heap collapsing in on itself and becoming slimy. Wine corks, party hats, cracker jokes, and streamers can also be added to the compost heap, as can tissue paper, which biodegrades quickly. Cardboard packaging from food and gifts can also be composted—both corrugated cardboard and printed card are suitable (the inks used are non-toxic).

Check the base of the heap after several months and dig out any dark, well-rotted compost. Mix up the remaining matter with a fork, and water it if it seems dry; if the heap is too wet, add some dry, bulky material. Acidic conditions inhibit decomposition, so occasionally add a little ground limestone or gardener's lime.

## Food waste facts

- **It is estimated** that three million tonnes of waste is generated over the festive period in the UK, but we'll recycle just 12 percent of that amount. Festive waste currently produced across the UK is predicted to be enough to fill 400,000 double-decker buses.

- **15,000 tonnes of Brussels sprouts** are bought in the UK during the Christmas period—the same weight as 37 jumbo jets—generating a huge quantity of compostable vegetable peelings.

- **Over 24 million glass jars** of mincemeat, pickles and cranberry sauce will be consumed over the festive period and if all these jars were recycled, it would save enough energy to boil water for 60 million cups of tea.

## Organic material to compost

- Vegetable and fruit peelings
- Tea leaves and coffee grounds
- Crushed egg shells
- Grass cuttings and weeds
- Paper, paper towels and newspaper
- Leaves from non-coniferous trees and shrubs
- Woody prunings
- Straw, hay, wool, sawdust and pets' bedding
- Vacuum dust
- Wood ash

Avoid meat, fish and cooked food, weed seeds, diseased plant material, disposable nappies, glossy newsprint, and coal ash.

# Dried fruit snacks

If you have an excess of fresh apples and pears in your pantry, an ideal way of preserving them to eat later is to dehydrate them. The dried fruits, which are high in fiber, vitamins, and complex carbohydrates, make an excellent snack food. They can either be air-dried, or left in a conventional oven to dry out. Dry orange slices in the same way to use as tree decorations.

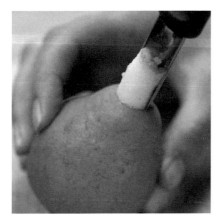

## ingredients

Preheat the oven to 120°F (49°C)

- 3.5 pints (1 liter) water
- 1 tsp salt or a little lemon juice
- Ripe apples and pears
- Several bamboo canes, or a length of string

**1** Pour the water into a large bowl and add the salt or lemon juice. You may need a second bowl of water if you have a lot of fruit. Then core each of the fruits.

**2** Slice the whole fruits into rings by cutting cross the cored center. Then add the slices to the salted water immediately to prevent them turning too brown.

## 🌿 Cooking tip

After 1 hour of cooking, increase the oven temperature to 140°F (60°C). Leave the oven door slightly open to prevent a build-up of condensation.

**3** Immerse the slices in the water. To air-dry the fruit, thread the slices onto bamboo canes or string and hang in front of an open fire until the fruits have completely dried out.

**4** To oven-dry the fruits, pat dry, arrange in a single layer on some cheesecloth on a rack, leave in oven for 1 hour, adjust the temperature, and leave for 3–6 hours until dry.

# Fabric garland

See pages 28–33. Make templates of the shapes that you like and cut out two of each shape, except for the robin's body and beak, for which you should cut out one of each shape, and the holly leaf, for which you should cut out four shapes.

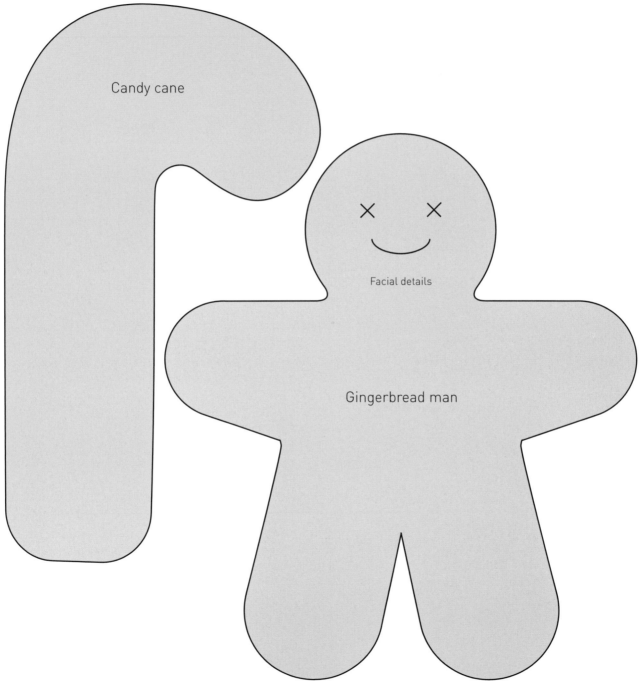

Candy cane

Facial details

Gingerbread man

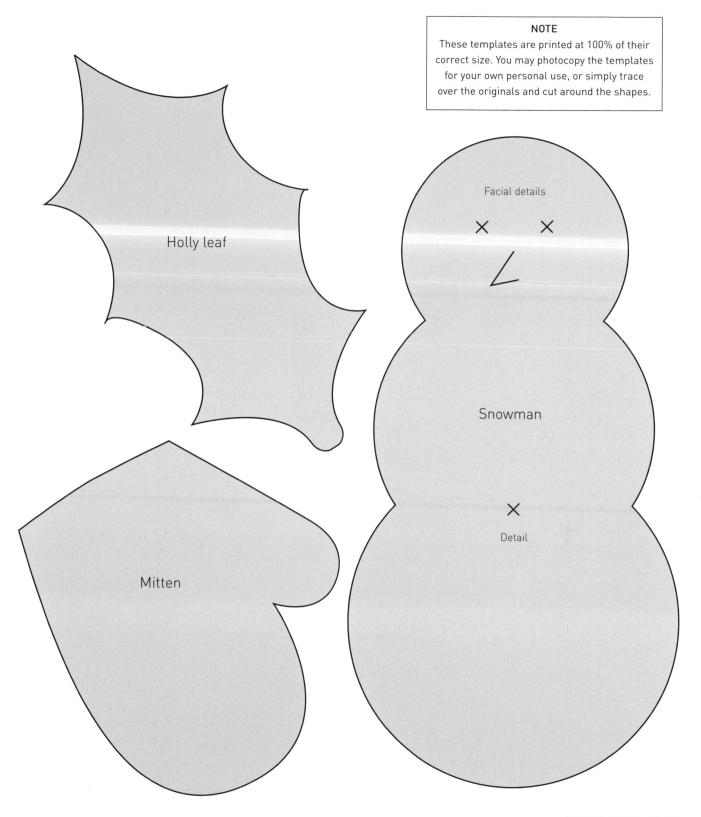

NOTE

These templates are printed at 100% of their correct size. You may photocopy the templates for your own personal use, or simply trace over the originals and cut around the shapes.

Holly leaf

Facial details

Snowman

Detail

Mitten

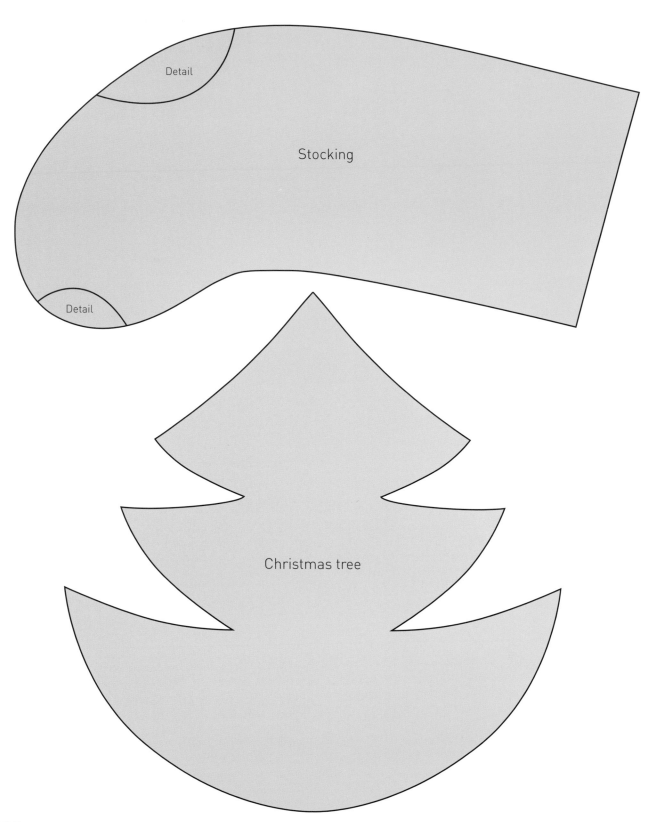

Detail

Detail

Stocking

Christmas tree

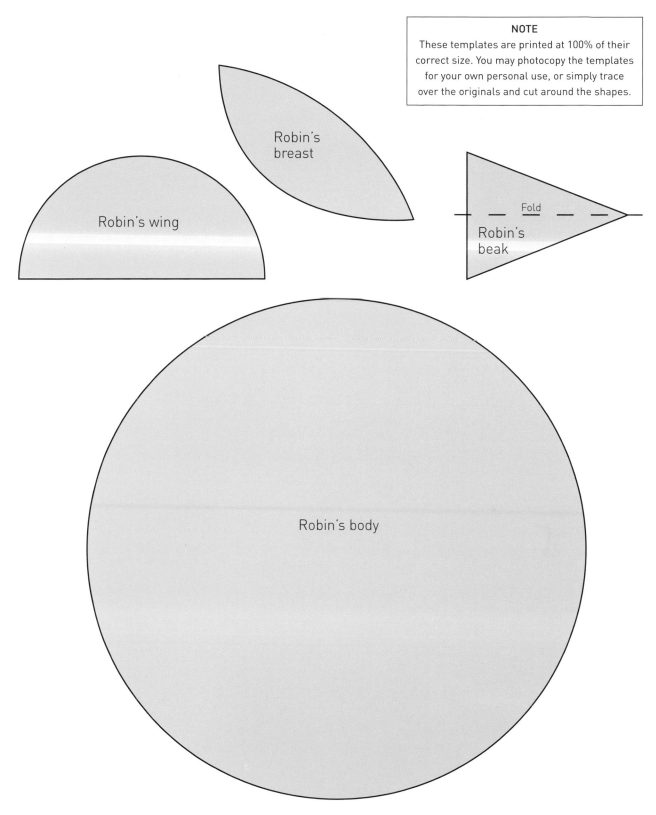

Robin's breast

**NOTE**
These templates are printed at 100% of their correct size. You may photocopy the templates for your own personal use, or simply trace over the originals and cut around the shapes.

Robin's wing

Fold

Robin's beak

Robin's body

# Doll pin tree angel

See pages 70–71. Make up the templates and cut out two angel dress shapes in fabric and one wing shape in felt.

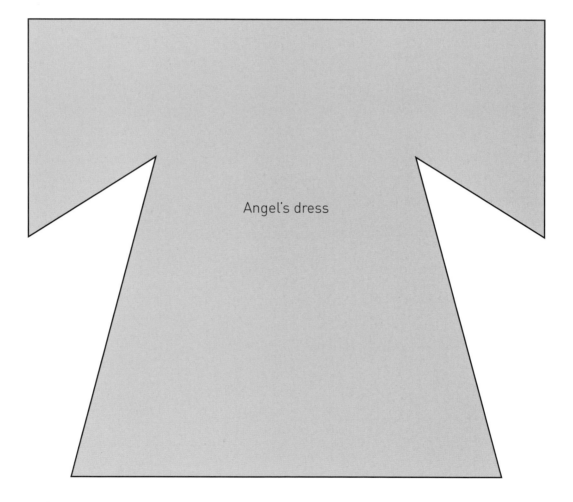

Angel's dress

Angel wings

# Festive birds

See pages 72–73. For each bird, make up the templates and cut out two body shapes, two wing shapes, and several flowers and leaves.

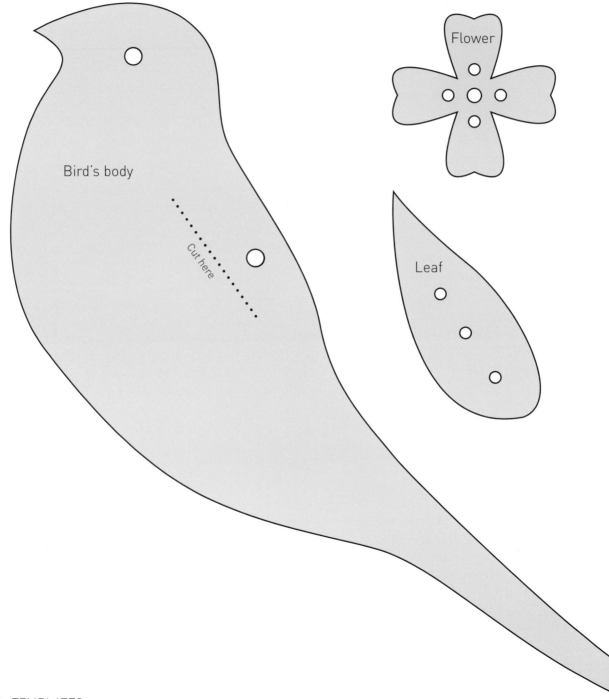

Flower

Bird's body

Cut here

Leaf

Bird wings

Cut here

Cut here

# Paper and fabric cards and decorations

See pages 76–77, 138–39, and 148–49.

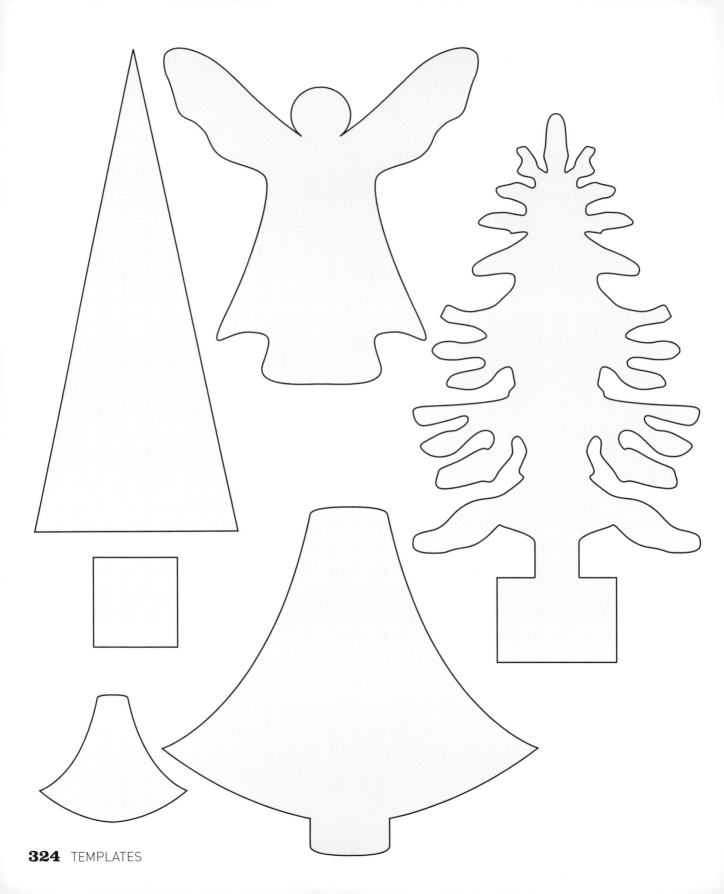

# Scented fabric hearts

See pages 78–79. For each fabric heart, cut two shapes from the template.

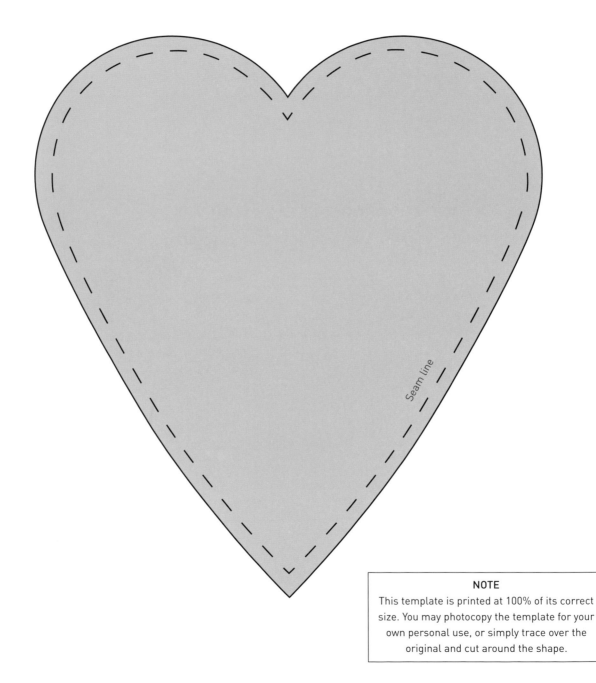

Seam line

**NOTE**

This template is printed at 100% of its correct size. You may photocopy the template for your own personal use, or simply trace over the original and cut around the shape.

# Candy cane cones

See pages 80–81. For each cone, cut out one felt shape and one fabric shape from the template.

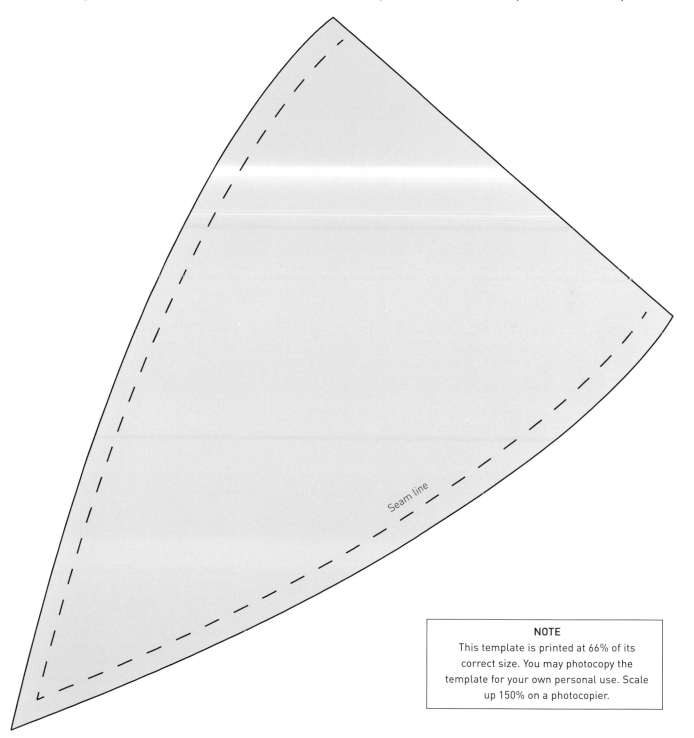

_Seam line_

**NOTE**
This template is printed at 66% of its correct size. You may photocopy the template for your own personal use. Scale up 150% on a photocopier.

# Advent calendar sacks

See pages 92–93. For each sack, cut out two shapes from the template.

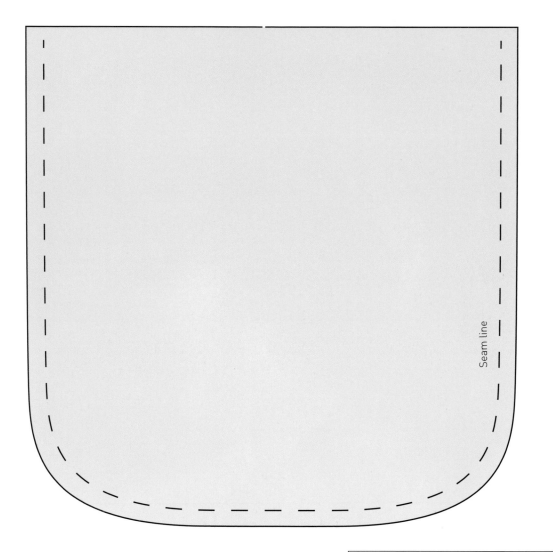

Seam line

**NOTE**
This template is printed at 100% of its correct size. You may photocopy the template for your own personal use, or simply trace over the original and cut around the shape.

# Stocking Advent calendar

See pages 94–95. For each stocking, cut out two shapes from the template.

**NOTE**
This template is printed at 100% of its correct size. You may photocopy the template for your own personal use, or simply trace over the original and cut around the shape.

# Christmas stocking

See pages 104–05. For each stocking, cut out two shapes from the template.

Seam line

# Hot-water bottle cover

See pages 118–19. For each hot-water bottle cover, cut out one shape from the front cover template, and one shape from each of the back cover templates. Cut out two shapes from either the heart or star template.

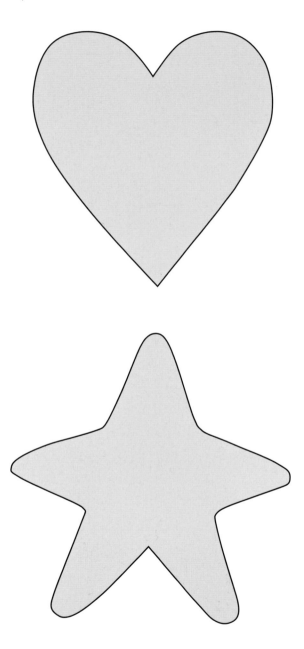

Front cover

Top back cover

Bottom back cover

# Felt slippers

See pages 180–81. Adjust the template sizes according to the foot size you want to make. Cut out one shape from each of the upper templates, and three shapes from each of the foot templates.

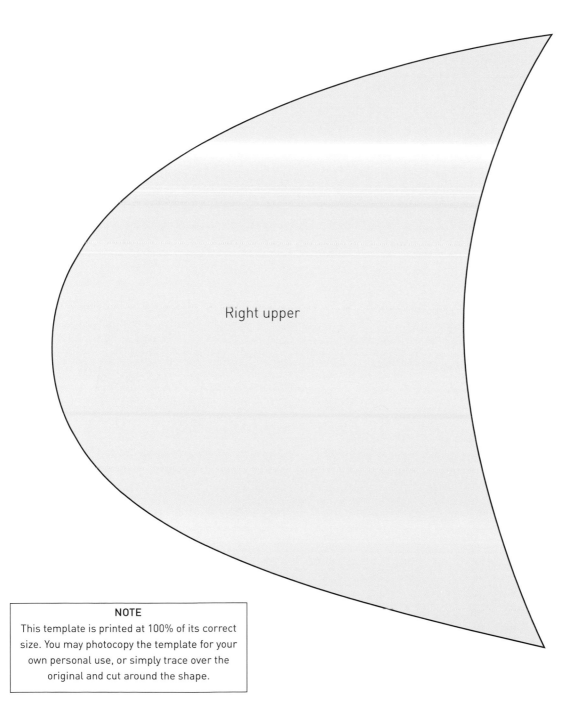

Right upper

**NOTE**
This template is printed at 100% of its correct size. You may photocopy the template for your own personal use, or simply trace over the original and cut around the shape.

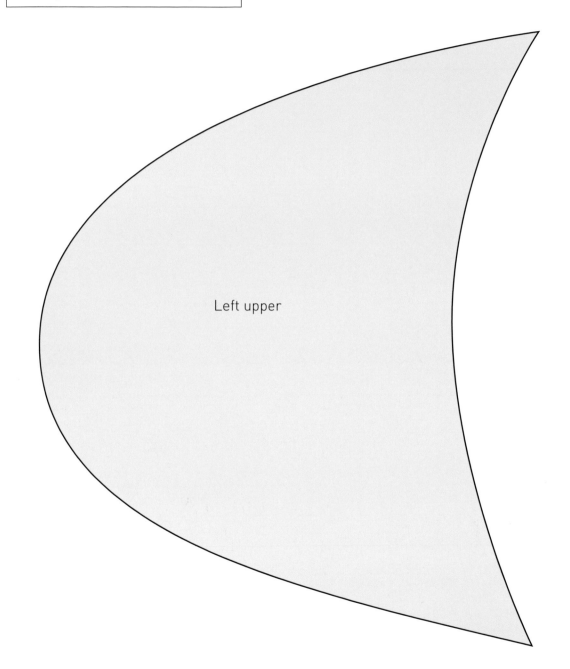

Left upper

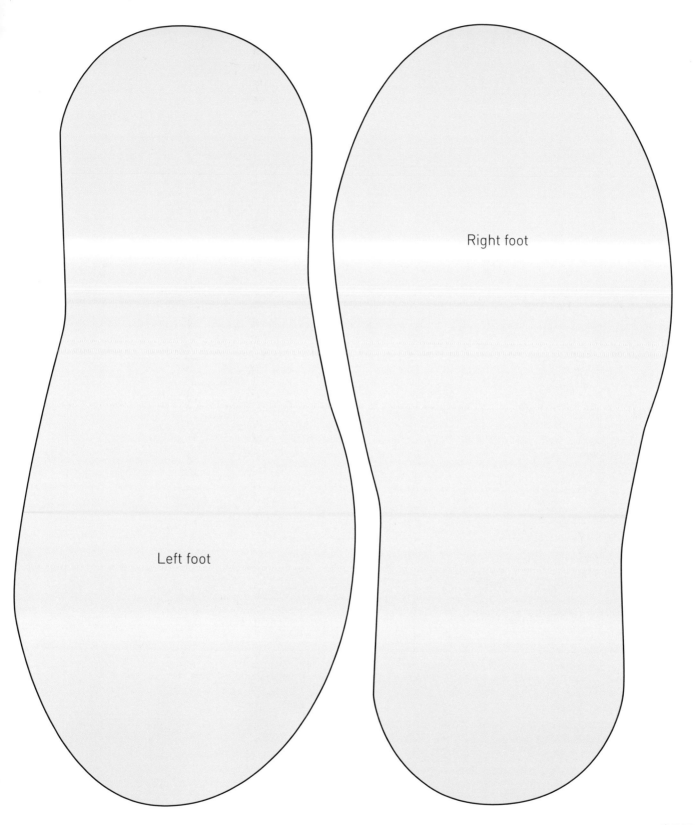

Right foot

Left foot

# Dried herb and moth-repellent sachets

See pages 150–51, and pages 154–55. For each sachet, cut out two shapes from the template.

Seam line

# Chicken doorstop

See pages 158–59. For each doorstop, cut two shapes from the body, head, and base templates, and one shape from the wattle and comb template.

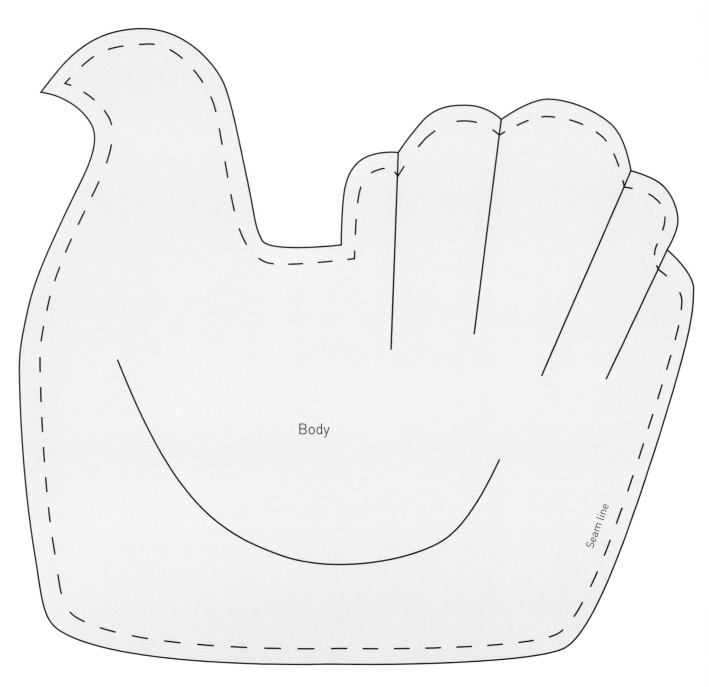

Body

Seam line

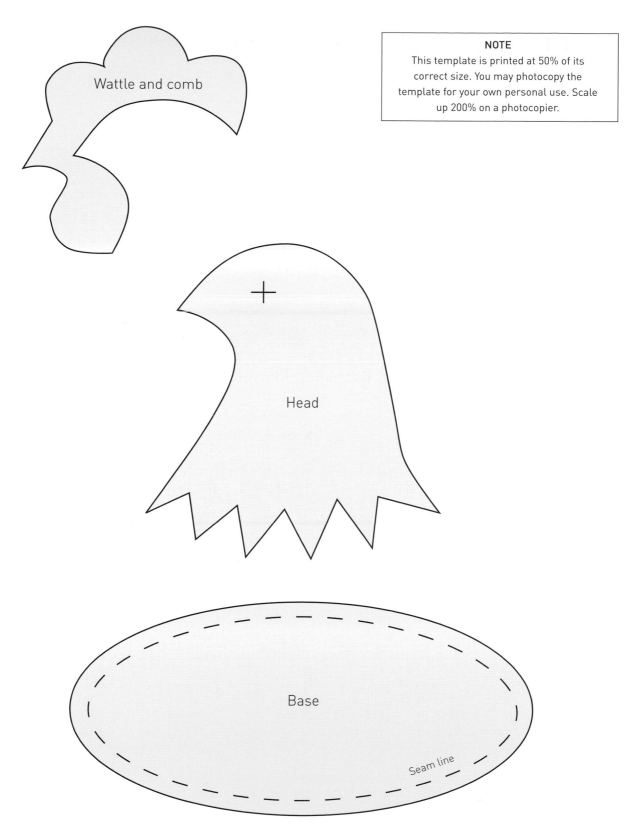

Wattle and comb

Head

Base

Seam line

# Cotton bag

See pages 170–73. Cut out four shapes from the bag template, and two shapes from the base template.

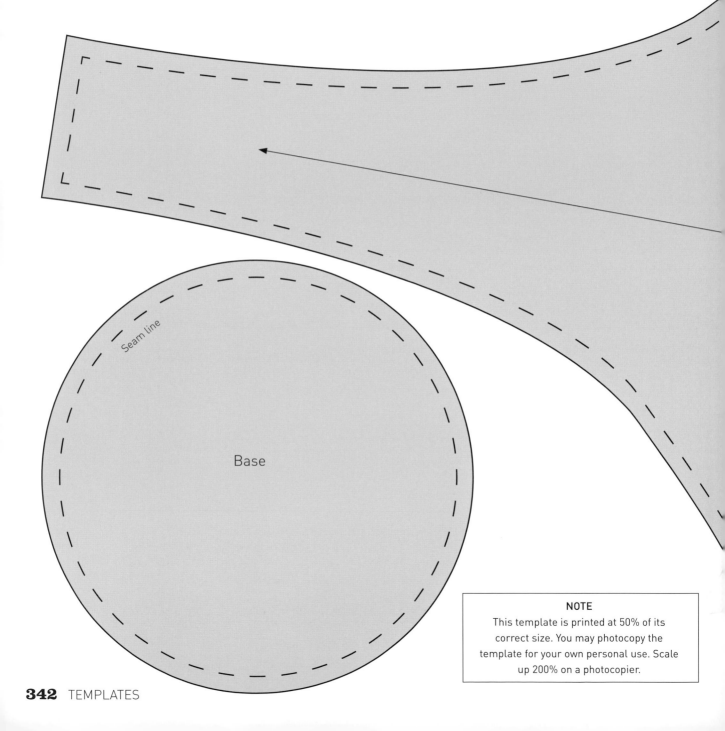

Seam line

Base

**NOTE**
This template is printed at 50% of its correct size. You may photocopy the template for your own personal use. Scale up 200% on a photocopier.

Seam line

Bag

Grainline

# Directory

## Crafts—General

**American Craft Council**
72 Spring Street
New York, NY 10012-4019
Tel: (212) 274-0630
Fax: (212) 274-0650
council@craftcouncil.org
www.craftcouncil.org

**Craftster**
Online crafting community with tips,
techniques, and clever ideas.
www.craftster.org

**Etsy**
Online resource for buying
handmade items, crafting materials,
and classes.
www.etsy.com

## Crafting materials

### For paint

**Old Fashioned Milk Paint Co.**
436 Main Street
Groton, MA 01450
Tel: (866) 350-6455
Fax: (978) 448-6336
www.milkpaint.com

**YOLO Colorhouse**
116 SE Yamhill Street
Portland, OR 97214
Tel: (877) 493-8275
Fax: (877) 232-0455
info@yolocolorhouse.com
www.yolocolorhouse.com

### For fabrics

**Reprodepot**
Tel: (413) 527-4047
Fax: (413) 527-6407
**reprodepot.com**
Online retailer selling fabrics,
ribbons, and trim

**Plover Organic**
www. ploverorganic.com
Organic fabric sold by the yard

### For paper

**EcoPaper**
1860 Eastman Avenue, Suite 101
Ventura, CA 93003
Tel: (805) 644-4462
www.ecopaper.com

**Living Tree Paper Company**
1430 Willamette Street, Suite 367
Eugene, OR 97401
Tel: (541) 342-2974
Fax: (541) 687-7744
info@livingtreepaper.com
www.livingtreeper

### For eco-friendly glue

**Amazing Ecoglue**
www.eclecticproducts.com/ecoglue

**Weldbond Vegan All-Purpose Glue**
www.ethicalplanet.com

### For donated gifts (life-saving equipment given to people in developing countries)

**Save the Children**
2000 L Street NW, Suite 500
Washington, DC 20036
Tel: (202) 640-6600
www.savethechildren.org

**World Wildlife Fund (WWF)**
1250 24th Street, NW
PO Box 97180
Washington, DC 20090-7180
Tel: (202) 293-4800
www.wwf.org

### For dulse seaweed

**Mendocino Sea Vegetable Company**
PO Box 455
Philo, CA 95466
Tel: (707) 895-2996
kombuko@seaweed.net
www.seaweed.net

### For organic lavender

**Hood River Lavender Farms**
PO Box 389
Odell, OR 97044
Tel: 1-888-LAV-FARM
info@lavenderfarms.net
www.lavenderfarms.net

**Leelanau Lavender Breezes**
9981 East Johnson Road
Northport, MI 49670
Tel: (231) 386-9256
erice@starband.net
www.leelanaulavender.com

**Olympic Lavender Farm**
1432 Marine Drive
Sequim, WA 98382
Tel: (360) 683-4475
info@olympiclavender.com
www.olympiclavender.com

### For powdered kelp

**Maine Coast Sea Vegetables**
3 George's Pond Road
Franklin, ME 04634
Tel: (207) 565-2907
Fax: (207) 565-2144
info@seaveg.com
www.seaveg.com

**Mountain Rose Herbs**
PO Box 50220
Eugene, OR 97405
Tel: (800) 879-3337
Fax: (510) 217-4012
www.mountainroseherbs.com

**Starwest Botanicals**
11253 Trade Center Drive
Rancho Cordova, CA 95742
www.starwest-botanicals.com

*For wild bird seed*

**Wild Birds Unlimited**
11711 N. College Avenue, Suite 146
Carmel, IN 46032
Tel: (800) 326-4928
Fax: (317) 571-7110
www.wbu.com

*For miniature galvanized buckets*

**Bucket outlet**
1035 Sylvatus Highway
Hillsville, VA 24343
Tel: 1-800-251-8824
Fax: (276) 728-5885
sales@redhillgeneralstore.com
www.bucket-outlet.com

# Food and drink

*Eat Grub*
www.eatgrub.org
Information on local, sustainable food

**Local Harvest**
www.localharvest.org
Searchable database of local farms,
farmer's markets, and restaurants
that support local suppliers.

**TransFair USA**
1500 Broadway, Suite 400
Oakland, CA 94612
Tel: (510) 663-5260
Fax: (510) 663-5264
info@transfairusa.org
www.transfairusa.org
Certifier of Fair Trade products

*To find inspected and accredited
local farmers' markets*

**Farmers Market Dot Com**
farmersmarket.com

**USDA database of farmers markets**
www.ams.usda.gov/farmersmarkets

**British Columbia Association of
Farmers' Markets**
www.bcfarmersmarket.org

**Farmers' Markets Ontario**
54 Bayshore Road
Brighton, ON K0K 1H0
Canada
Tel: 1-800-387-3276
Fax: (613) 475-2913
fmo@farmersmarketsontario.com
www.farmersmarketsontario.com

*A selection of farmers' markets*

Cortelyou Farmers Market
Cortelyou Road
Brooklyn, NY 11226
Tel: (212) 788-7476
Fax: (212) 571-0778
info@greenmarket.cc
www.cenyc.org
(Brooklyn: New York)

**Farmers Market**
6333 West 3rd Street
Los Angeles, CA 90036
Tel: (323) 933-9211
Fax: (323) 549-2145
www.farmersmarketla.com
(Los Angeles: California)

**Minneapolis Farmers Market**
Attn: Market Manager
PO Box 2006
Inver Grove Heights, MN 55076
Tel: (612) 333-1718
Fax: (651) 457-3319
info@mplsfarmersmarket.com
www.mplsfarmersmarket.com

**Portland Farmers Market**
1001 SE Water Avenue, Suite 455
Portland, OR 97214
Tel: (503) 241-0032
Fax: (503) 241-2262
contact@portlandfarmersmarket.org
portlandfarmersmarket.org

**Union Square Green Market**
Broadway at 17th St
New York, NY 10011
(Manhattan: New York)

*To find out what produce is in season*

**Eating with the Seasons**
3739 Balboa Street, PMB 157
San Francisco, CA 94121
Tel: (831) 245-8125
Fax: (415) 520-6063
www.eatwiththeseasons.com

*For fruit and vegetable box deliveries*
*www.allorganiclinks.com*

**Absolute Organics**
www.theabsoluteorganics.com
sales@theabsoluteorganics.com
(Charlotte/Hickory: North Carolina)

**Brown Box Organics Company**
PO Box 9057
Nampa, ID 83652
Tel: (208) 362-5677

www.brownboxorganics.com
(Greater Boise area: Idaho)

**Door to Door Organics**
7036-D Easton Road
Pipersville, PA 18947
Tel: 1-888-283-4443
www.doortodoororganics.com
(Colorado, Michigan, Pennsylvania,
and Ohio River Valley)

**Papas Organic**
www.papasorganic.com
Tel: (866) SHOP-PAPAS
store@papasorganic.com
(Various locations)

**Planet Organics**
19449 Riverside Drive, Suite 100
Sonoma, CA 95476
Tel: (800) 956-5855
Fax: (707) 933-9178
service@planetorganics.com
www.planetorganics.com
(San Francisco/Bay Area: California)

**For organic meat**

**Diamond Organics**
1272 Highway 1
Moss Landing, CA 95039
Tel: 1-888-ORGANIC
www.diamondorganics.com

**Eberly Poultry**
1095 Mt. Airy Road
Stevens, PA 17578
Tel: (717) 336-6440
Fax: (717) 336-6905
www.eberlypoultry.com

**Lobel's Poultry**
1096 Madison Avenue
New York, NY 10028
Tel: (877) 783-4512
www.lobels.com

**Vermont Natural Beef**
1943 Stage Road
Benson, VT 05743
Tel: (802) 537-3711
www.vermontnaturalbeef.com

**For organic flour**

**Bob's Red Mill Natural Foods**
13521 SE Pheasant Court
Milwaukie, OR 97222
Tel: 1-800-349-2173
www.bobsredmill.com

**Eden Organic**
701 Tecumseh Road
Clinton, MI 49236
Tel: 888-424-EDEN
www.edenfoods.com

**Dakota Prairie Organic
Flour Company**
500 North Street West
Harvey, ND 58341
Tel: (701) 324-4330

Fax: (701) 324-4334
www.dakota-prairie.com

**Fairhaven Organic Flour Mill**
www.fairhavenflour.com

**For organic gin**

**The Organic Spirit Co.**
www.junipergreen.org

**For wild foods**

**Wild Food Plants**
wildfoodplants.com

# Home

**A Natural Home**
www.anaturalhome.com

**For babies and children**

**Green Nest**
18662 MacArthur Boulevard
Suite 200
Irvine, CA 92612
Tel: (888) 473-6466
Fax: (949) 387.3806
support@greennest.com
www.greennest.com

**Natural Pod**
PO Box 147
Cobble Hill, BC V0R-1L0
Canada
Tel: (604) 630-1619
info@naturalpod.com
www.naturalpod.com

**Sage Baby**
Tel: (917) 930-1852
info@sagebabynyc.com
www.sagebabynyc.com

**For bath towels**

**Ecobathrooms**
www.ecobathroom.com

**For eco-friendly household products**

**EcoMall**
www.ecomall.com

**Ecover**
www.ecover.com

**Kokopelli's Green Market**
PO Box 353
Brandon, VT 05733
Tel: (800) 210-0202
Fax: (802) 247-4114

CustomerService@KokoGM.com
www.KokoGM.com

**Seventh Generation**
60 Lake Street
Burlington, VT 05401X
Tel: (800) 456-1191
Fax: (802) 658-1771
www.seventhgeneration.com

**For energy-efficient Christmas lights**

**Holiday LEDs**
Tel: (888) 430-6551
HolidayLEDs.com

**Inirgee.com**
PO Box 324
Belleville, KS 66935
Tel: (615) 826-7324
Fax: (866) 240-2706
info@inirgee.com
www.inirgee.com

**For sustainable wood furniture**

**Sustainable Woods Network**
Tel: (608) 347-8400
info@sustainablewoods.net
www.sustainablewoods.net

**For recycled and vintage products (to buy or sell)**

**The Freecycle Network**
PO Box 294
Tucson, AZ 85702
info@freecycle.org
www.freecycle.org

**For information on cleaner wood burning stoves and fireplaces**

**US Environmental Protection Agency**
www.epa.gov/woodstoves/

**For organic cotton clothing**

**Cottonfield USA**
19 Braintree Street, Suite 312
Boston, MA 02134
Tel: (888) 954-1551
Fax: (617) 787-8112
customerservice@cottonfieldusa.com
www.cottonfieldusa.com

*For vintage tablecloths*

**The Vintage Table**
www.thevintagetable.net

# Garden

**The National Christmas Tree Association**
16020 Swingley Ridge Road, Suite 300
Chesterfield, MO 63017
Tel: (636) 449-5070
Fax: (636) 449-5051
info@realchristmastrees.org
www.christmastree.org

**Forest Stewardship Council**
www.fsc.org

*For living Christmas trees*

**Living Christmas Trees**
Rent a Christmas tree that will be delivered to you, picked up after New Year's, and planted
www.livingchristmastrees.org

*For advice on composting*

www.composters.com
www.homeharvest.com

**Composting Council of Canada**
16, rue Northumberland Street
Toronto, ON  M6H 1P7
Canada
Tel: (416) 535-0240
Fax: (416) 536-9892
ccc@compost.org
www.compost.org

**US Composting Council**
1 Comac Loop, Suite 14B1
Ronkonkoma, NY 11779
Tel: (631) 737-4931
Fax: (631) 737-4939
admin@compostingcouncil.org
www.compostingcouncil.org

*For organic gardening supplies*
www.gardensalive.com
www.greenpromise.com

*For organic seeds*

**Main Street Seed & Supply Company**
Bay Farm Services, Inc.
401 Main Street
Bay City, MI 48706
Tel: 1-866-229-3276
service@mainstreetseedandsupply.com
www.mainstreetseedandsupply.com

**Park Seed Company**
www.parkseed.com

**Seeds of Change**
Tel: 1-888-762-7333
www.seedsofchange.com

*For a grow-your-own mistletoe kit*

**Mistle**
www.mistle.co.uk (for booklet)

**Tenbury English Mistletoe Enterprise**
www.tenbury-mistletoe.co.uk

# Recycling and saving energy

*For information on Christmas card recycling schemes*

**CardsDirect Card Recycling and Re-Use Program**
200 Chisholm Place, Suite 220
Plano, TX 75075

**The Greeting Card Recycling Program at St. Jude's Ranch for Children**
100 St. Jude's Street
Boulder City, NV 89005-1681

*For information on New York City-based collection and mulching of live trees in January*

**MULCHFEST**
www.nycgovparks.org/services/mulchfest/mulchfest.html

*For links to sites on recycling your holiday waste*
**www.earth911.org**
*For information on recycling anything from batteries to bicycles*

**Friends of the Earth**
1717 Massachusetts Avenue, Suite 600
Washington, DC 20036
Tel: (202) 783-7400
Fax: (202) 783-0444
www.foe.org

**National Recycling Coalition**
www.nrc-recycle.org

**Recycler's World**
www.recycle.net

**Recycling Council of British Columbia**
Suite 10-119 W. Pender Street
Vancouver, BC V6B 1S5
Canada
Tel: (800) 667-4321
www.rcbc.bc.ca

**Recycling Council of Ontario**
215 Spadina Avenue  #407
Toronto, ON M5T 2C7
Canada
Tel: (416) 657-2797
www.rco.on.ca

**United States Environmental Protection Agency (EPA)**
Ariel Rios Building
1200 Pennsylvania Avenue, NW
Washington, DC 20460
www.epa.gov

*For tips and advice on how to reduce your carbon footprint*

www.carbonfund.org
www.carbonfootprint.com
www.conservation.org

*For advice on saving energy*

**US Department of Energy Efficiency and Renewable Energy**
www.eere.enery.gov

# Index